LOVE
SHOULDN'T
HURT

BREAKING THE CHAINS OF
DOMESTIC VIOLENCE

BENJAMIN HOLLAND

Ordering Information:

Prime Seven Media
518 Landmann St.
Tomah City, WI 54660

Printed in the United States of America

Table of Contents

Introduction 1

Understanding Domestic Violence 3

Chapter 1 11

Chapter 2 12

Chapter 3 14

Chapter 4 16

Chapter 5 21

Chapter 6 23

Chapter 7 25

Chapter 8 27

Chapter 9 30

Chapter 10 32

Chapter 11 34

Chapter 12 37

Chapter 13 39

Chapter 14 41

Chapter 15 43

Chapter 16 45

Chapter 17 47

Chapter 18 50

Chapter 19 52

Chapter 20 54

Chapter 21 56

Chapter 22 58

Chapter 23 60

Chapter 24 62

Chapter 25 64

Chapter 26 66

Chapter 27 69

Chapter 28 71

Chapter 29 73

Chapter 30 75

Chapter 31 77

Chapter 32 79

Chapter 33 81

Chapter 34 84

Chapter 35 86

Chapter 36 89

Chapter 37 92

Chapter 38 94

Chapter 39 96

Chapter 40 98

Chapter 41 101

Chapter 42 104

Chapter 43 107

Chapter 44 110

Chapter 45 113

Chapter 46 115

Chapter 47 117

Chapter 48 120

Chapter 49 122

Chapter 50 124

Chapter 51 126

Chapter 52 129

Chapter 53 132

Chapter 54 134

Chapter 55 136

Chapter 56 138

Chapter 57 140

Chapter 58 143

Chapter 59 145

Chapter 60 147

Chapter 61 149

Chapter 62 151

Chapter 63 153

Chapter 64 155

Chapter 65 158

Chapter 66 160

Chapter 67 162

Chapter 68 168

Conclusion...171

Synopsis 173

About the Author 177

Introduction

In a world that cherishes love and compassion, it is a devastating reality that countless individuals find themselves trapped in the cycle of domestic violence. Behind closed doors, where shadows conceal the scars and tears go unheard, a sinister force shatters the very essence of what love should be. It is within this darkness that our journey begins, as we explore the unspoken truths and untold stories of those who have dared to confront and overcome the harrowing specter of abuse.

"Love Shouldn't Hurt" is not just a book; it is a guiding light that seeks to illuminate the hidden corners of an epidemic that spans across cultures, socio-economic boundaries, and generations. With empathy as our compass, we embark on a voyage that will unravel the tangled web of domestic violence, revealing the multifaceted layers of its impact on individuals, families, and communities.

Within these pages, you will bear witness to the raw and unfiltered narratives of survivors who have summoned the courage to break free from the suffocating grip of violence. Their stories will ignite a fire within your soul, dispelling the misconceptions that shroud domestic abuse in silence and shame. Through their resilience and determination, we will uncover the strength that lies within each survivor and the power of collective support in the face of adversity.

"Love Shouldn't Hurt" transcends the boundaries of victimhood, offering a comprehensive understanding of the complex dynamics

that perpetuate domestic violence. We delve into the psychological, emotional, and physical aspects of abuse, shedding light on the warning signs, the manipulative tactics employed by abusers, and the long-lasting trauma experienced by survivors.

But this book is not solely about the darkness; it is a beacon of hope, fostering empowerment and inspiring change. It serves as a rallying cry for a society that refuses to turn a blind eye but instead stands united against the scourge of domestic violence. Together, we will explore avenues for prevention, education, and support, illuminating a path towards healing and a future where love truly becomes a sanctuary, untainted by violence.

"Love Shouldn't Hurt" is a call to action, a testament to the resilience of the human spirit, and a catalyst for change. As you embark on this transformative journey, may you find solace, understanding, and the unwavering belief that love should never be a source of pain.

Understanding Domestic Violence

By Benjamin Holland

D omestic violence is a pervasive issue that affects individuals of all backgrounds, genders, and ages. It is characterized by a pattern of abusive behavior that is used by one partner to gain power and control over the other. Domestic violence can take many forms, including physical, emotional, sexual, and financial abuse, and can have long-lasting physical, emotional, and psychological effects on its victims.

The phrase *"Love Shouldn't Hurt"* is often used in the context of domestic violence awareness and prevention. It highlights the idea that love is meant to be a positive and nurturing force in a relationship and that any form of violence or abuse is not acceptable. Domestic violence is not a normal part of a healthy relationship, and we must educate ourselves about the warning signs and take action to prevent it.

Physical abuse is perhaps the most well-known form of domestic violence, and it can take many forms, including hitting, pushing, slapping, choking, and using weapons. However, domestic violence can also include emotional and psychological abuse, such as verbal insults, threats, and isolation from friends and family. Sexual abuse can involve forcing a partner to engage in sexual activity without their consent or using coercion or manipulation to get them to comply. Financial abuse involves controlling a partner's access to money and resources, which can prevent them from leaving an abusive situation.

One of the most challenging aspects of domestic violence is that it often occurs in secret, behind closed doors. Victims may feel ashamed or embarrassed and may fear retaliation from their abuser if they try to leave. This is why it is so important to create a culture of awareness and support, where victims feel safe and empowered to speak out and seek help.

If you or someone you know is experiencing domestic violence, it is important to reach out for help. There are many resources available, including hotlines, shelters, and counseling services, that can provide support and guidance. It is also important to hold abusers accountable for their actions, through legal means if necessary.

In conclusion, domestic violence is a serious issue that affects individuals and families around the world. The phrase "*Love Shouldn't Hurt*" emphasizes the importance of recognizing the warning signs of abuse, and taking action to prevent it. By educating ourselves and creating a culture of awareness and support, we can work towards a world where all individuals are treated with respect and dignity, and where love truly does not hurt.

Subjects of the next chapters consist of:

Bringing old baggage into new relationships refers to the tendency of people to carry emotional baggage from past relationships into new ones. This baggage can include unresolved issues, past hurt or trauma, negative beliefs, and unhealthy patterns of behavior.

When people bring old baggage into new relationships, it can negatively impact the new relationship. For example, a person who has been hurt in the past may be overly guarded or defensive in their new relationship, which can make it difficult for them to fully open up and trust their new partner. Similarly, a person who has experienced betrayal in the past may be overly suspicious or jealous in their new relationship, which can create tension and conflict. To avoid bringing old baggage into new relationships, it's important to take time to reflect on past experiences and to work through any unresolved emotions or issues. This may involve seeking support from a therapist or counselor, talking with trusted friends or family members, or engaging in self-reflection and personal growth activities It's also important to communicate openly and honestly with your new partner about your past experiences and any concerns or fears you may have about the relationship. This can help to build trust and establish a strong foundation for a healthy and fulfilling relationship.

Insecure boyfriends or girlfriends. Insecurity is a common issue that can arise in romantic relationships. Insecure boyfriends or girlfriends may exhibit behaviors such as jealousy, possessiveness, neediness, and constant reassurance-seeking from their partners. Insecurity can stem from a variety of factors, such as past experiences of rejection or abandonment, low self-esteem, anxiety, or a lack of trust in oneself or others. Insecure individuals may also project their insecurities onto their partner, assuming that their partner is not fully committed or interested in the relationship. While it's natural for everyone to experience some level of insecurity at times, excessive insecurity can be damaging to a relationship. It can lead to feelings of suffocation, resentment, and frustration for the partner who is on the receiving end of the insecurity. If you are in a relationship with an insecure partner, it's important to communicate openly and honestly with them about your feelings and concerns. Encourage your partner to work on their insecurities by seeking support from a therapist or counselor, engaging in self-reflection and personal growth activities, and building their self-esteem. It's also important to set boundaries and maintain your sense of independence within the relationship. This can help to prevent your partner's insecurity from becoming overwhelming and allow both partners to feel respected and valued in the relationship.

Learn who you're getting into a relationship with about background checks etc. As an AI language model, I do not have a personal opinion, but I can provide you with some information that may help you make an informed decision. It is natural to want to learn more about a person you are interested in dating, especially if you are considering a serious relationship. However, it is important to approach this respectfully and ethically. Background checks can potentially provide a lot of information about a person's past, including criminal records, employment history, financial information, and more. However, it is important to keep in mind that there are legal and ethical considerations to take into account. In many countries, it is illegal to conduct a background check on someone without their knowledge or consent. Additionally, even if it is legal, it can be seen as a violation of trust and privacy if someone conducts a background check without the other person's knowledge. Instead of conducting a background check, it may be more appropriate to get to know the person by spending time together and having open and honest conversations. You can ask them about their interests, goals, values, and past experiences to get a better understanding of who they are. Ultimately, the decision of whether or not to conduct a background check is up to you. However, it is important to consider the legal and ethical implications and to approach the situation with respect and sensitivity.

Understanding red flags as it relates to acknowledging signs of domestic violence tendencies. Red flags are warning signs that may indicate the presence of domestic violence tendencies in an individual. These red flags can be observed in their behavior, attitudes, and actions.

Some common red flags to look out for include:

1. **Controlling behavior:** This could manifest in the form of constantly monitoring the victim's activities, isolating them from friends and family, or insisting on making all decisions for them.

2. **Jealousy:** An abuser may become jealous of minor interactions with others, or accuse the victim of cheating or flirting.

3. **Blaming:** Abusers may often blame their victims for any issues in the relationship and refuse to take responsibility for their actions.

4. **Mood swings:** Abusers may exhibit extreme mood swings, becoming angry or violent over small things.

5. **Verbal abuse:** This can include name-calling, insults, and making threats.

6. **Intimidation**: An abuser may use intimidation tactics such as smashing objects, throwing things, or making threatening gestures.

7. **Physical violence:** This is the most obvious red flag, but it may not always be present at the beginning of a relationship.

It is important to note that not all abusers exhibit all of these red flags, and some may be more subtle than others. It is also important to remember that not all individuals who exhibit these red flags will become abusers. However, if you notice any of these signs in someone you know, it is important to take them seriously and seek help if necessary.

When you tell someone that you love them but it only means to get to have sex with them. Telling someone that you love them just to have sex with them is manipulative and disingenuous behavior. Love is a complex emotion that involves caring for someone deeply and wanting the best for them. Using the word "love" to manipulate someone into having sex with you is dishonest and can cause emotional harm to the other person. It's important, to be honest and respectful in any kind of relationship and to make sure that both parties are on the same page about what their intentions are. If you are only interested in a sexual relationship, it's important to communicate that clearly and honestly, without leading the other person on or making false promises. And also telling someone that you love them and only means just have sex with them but they're controlling aspect that they won't tell you about. mental issues from your childhood that you didn't explain to your partner. I would want to Explain any personal experiences or emotions, that I had In regards to mental issues. However, it is important to note that if you are struggling with mental health issues from your childhood or at any point in your life, it is important to seek help from a mental health professional who can provide you with the support and tools you need to address and manage your symptoms. It is also up to you to decide when and how to share your experiences with your partner, but it can be helpful to communicate with them about your feelings and experiences in a supportive and understanding environment.

Relationships that only pertain to friends with benefits. Friends-with-benefits relationships typically involve a sexual component but are not considered romantic or committed partnerships. Therefore, the types of relationships that pertain to friends with benefits are generally limited to physical intimacy and casual friendship, without the emotional attachment and expectations of a traditional romantic relationship. Some common characteristics of friends-with-benefits relationships might include: Casual sex: The primary focus of the relationship is sexual activity, without the expectation of romantic involvement or commitment. Limited emotional attachment: While friends-with-benefits partners may enjoy each other's company and share some level of emotional intimacy, there is typically less emotional attachment than in a committed relationship. No exclusivity: Friends-with-benefits relationships usually do not involve exclusivity or monogamy, and partners may have other sexual partners or dating relationships. Clear communication: Friends with benefits partners need to have clear communication about their expectations and boundaries to ensure that both parties are on the same page. Respect and mutual enjoyment: Even though the relationship may be casual, both partners need to treat each other with respect and ensure that both parties are enjoying the experience.

Domestic violence and adolescents: Domestic violence is a serious problem that affects individuals of all ages, including adolescents. Adolescent domestic violence involves violent or abusive behavior by one partner in an intimate relationship towards the other partner, where one or both partners are under the age of Adolescents who experience domestic violence may suffer physical, emotional, and psychological harm, which can have long-lasting effects on their well-being. They may also be at a higher risk of developing mental health issues such as depression, anxiety, and post-traumatic stress disorder (**PTSD**). Adolescents who witness domestic violence between their parents or caregivers may also experience negative consequences, such as increased anxiety, fear, and confusion. They may also be more likely to develop aggressive or violent behavior themselves and to experience difficulty forming healthy relationships in the future. It is important to recognize the signs of domestic violence in adolescents and to provide support and resources to help them escape abusive situations and begin the healing process. This can include counseling, legal advocacy, and shelter services. It is also important to educate adolescents about healthy relationships and to promote positive behaviors that can prevent domestic violence from occurring in the first place.

Chapter 1

C ontrolling men: Controlling behavior that involves lies and manipulation can be a form of emotional abuse, and it is not acceptable for anyone to try to control another person in this way. This can happen in any kind of relationship, including romantic relationships, friendships, family relationships, and professional relationships. If you or someone you know is experiencing this kind of behavior, it is important to seek help and support. This can include talking to a trusted friend or family member, seeking counseling or therapy, or reaching out to a support organization or hotline for guidance. It is also important to set boundaries with the person who is trying to control you and to prioritize your own mental and emotional well-being.

Chapter 2

Controlling women: Controlling women through manipulation is a form of emotional abuse and is never acceptable. It is important to recognize that everyone has the right to make their own choices and decisions, and no one should be forced or coerced into doing something that they do not want to do. Manipulation can take many forms, including gaslighting, guilt-tripping, or using threats or intimidation. It can be difficult to recognize manipulation when it is happening, especially if it is coming from someone you care about or trust. However, it is important to be aware of the signs of manipulation and to seek help if you feel like you are being controlled. If you or someone you know is experiencing manipulation or emotional abuse, there are resources available to help. You can reach out to a trusted friend or family member, a therapist, or a domestic violence hotline for support and guidance. It is important to prioritize your safety and well-being and to seek help if you need it. Manipulation in relationships: Manipulation in relationships refers to any behavior that is intended to control or influence another person's thoughts, feelings, or actions without their consent or understanding. It can take many different forms, such as emotional manipulation, gaslighting, or coercive control. Emotional manipulation involves using tactics like guilt, fear, or shame to manipulate a person's emotions and behavior. Gaslighting is a specific type of emotional manipulation where the manipulator tries to make the victim doubt their perceptions and memories. Coercive control involves using a pattern of behavior that is intended to dominate and control another person, often through threats, intimidation, or isolation. Manipulation in relationships can be extremely damaging and can lead to feelings of confusion, anxiety, and low self-esteem. It can also make it difficult for the victim to trust others and form healthy relationships in the future. If you believe that you are being manipulated in a relationship, it is important to seek help and support from a trusted friend, family member, or professional.

Chapter 3

S ex does not inherently play a major role in domestic violence. Domestic violence is a complex issue that involves various factors, including power dynamics, control, and abusive behavior. It is important to note that domestic violence can occur in relationships regardless of the individual's gender or sexual orientation.

However, gender can indeed be a significant factor in domestic violence due to societal norms, power imbalances, and cultural expectations. Historically, women have been more commonly identified as victims of domestic violence, and men have been more commonly identified as perpetrators. This is not to say that men cannot be victims or that women cannot be perpetrators, as domestic violence can happen in any relationship regardless of gender.

Sexual dynamics can intersect with domestic violence in several ways:

1. **Power and control:** In relationships where one partner seeks to exert power and control over the other, sex can be used as a tool for manipulation, coercion, or punishment. This can involve forcing or pressuring a partner into unwanted sexual activities or using sex as a means to maintain dominance and control.

2. **Stigmatization and shame:** Sexual abuse or assault can be used to demean, degrade, or humiliate a partner, causing emotional and psychological harm. This can include using derogatory language, engaging in non-consensual sexual acts, or making a partner feel ashamed or guilty about their sexuality.

3. **Barriers to seeking help:** Societal expectations and gender norms can create barriers for victims of domestic violence to seek help or report the abuse. For example, men may face stigma or disbelief when disclosing abuse, particularly if it involves sexual violence. This can make it more difficult for male victims to come forward and seek support.

4. **Economic dependence:** In some cases, financial or economic factors can contribute to the power dynamics in relationships. Economic dependence on an abusive partner can make it more challenging for victims to leave the abusive situation, including instances where sexual coercion or exploitation is present.

It is crucial to recognize that domestic violence is not solely related to sex or sexual dynamics. It is a multifaceted issue that involves various forms of abuse, including physical, emotional, psychological, and financial abuse. Addressing domestic violence requires a comprehensive approach that promotes healthy relationship dynamics, gender equality, and support for all individuals affected by abuse.

Chapter 4

Sex does not inherently play a major role in domestic violence. Domestic violence is a complex issue that involves various factors, including power dynamics, control, and abusive behavior. It is important to note that domestic violence can occur in relationships regardless of the individual's gender or sexual orientation.

However, gender can indeed be a significant factor in domestic violence due to societal norms, power imbalances, and cultural expectations. Historically, women have been more commonly identified as victims of domestic violence, and men have been more commonly identified as perpetrators. This is not to say that men cannot be victims or that women cannot be perpetrators, as domestic violence can happen in any relationship regardless of gender.

Sexual dynamics can intersect with domestic violence in several ways:

1. **Power and control:** In relationships where one partner seeks to exert power and control over the other, sex can be used as a tool for manipulation, coercion, or punishment. This can involve forcing or pressuring a partner into unwanted sexual activities or using sex as a means to maintain dominance and control.

2. **Stigmatization and shame:** Sexual abuse or assault can be used to demean, degrade, or humiliate a partner, causing emotional and psychological harm. This can include using derogatory language, engaging in non-consensual sexual acts, or making a partner feel ashamed or guilty about their sexuality.

3. **Barriers to seeking help:** Societal expectations and gender norms can create barriers for victims of domestic violence to seek help or report the abuse. For example, men may face stigma or disbelief when disclosing abuse, particularly if it involves sexual violence. This can make it more difficult for male victims to come forward and seek support.

4. **Economic dependence:** In some cases, financial or economic factors can contribute to the power dynamics in relationships. Economic dependence on an abusive partner can make it more challenging for victims to leave the abusive situation, including instances where sexual coercion or exploitation is present.

It is crucial to recognize that domestic violence is not solely related to sex or sexual dynamics. It is a multifaceted issue that involves various forms of abuse, including physical, emotional, psychological, and financial abuse. Addressing domestic violence requires a comprehensive approach that promotes healthy relationship dynamics, gender equality, and support for all individuals affected by abuse. Sex plays a complex role in relationships, and when it comes to domestic violence, it can intersect with various factors to contribute to the dynamics of abuse. It is important to note that domestic violence can occur in relationships regardless of the individual's gender or sexual orientation. However, gender-based factors often play a significant role in domestic violence due to societal norms, power imbalances, and cultural expectations.

Historically, women have been more commonly identified as victims of domestic violence, and men have been more commonly identified as perpetrators. This is not to say that men cannot be victims or that women cannot be perpetrators, as domestic violence can happen in any relationship regardless of gender. It is crucial to acknowledge that both men and women can be victims and that domestic violence can occur in same-sex relationships as well.

In the context of domestic violence, sex can influence the dynamics in several ways:

1. **Power and control:** Domestic violence is often rooted in power imbalances, where one partner seeks to exert control over the other. Sex can be used as a tool for manipulation, coercion, or punishment within an abusive relationship. For example, an abuser may use sexual violence or threats of sexual violence to maintain dominance and control over their partner.

2. **Sexual coercion and exploitation:** In abusive relationships, one partner may use various tactics to coerce the other into unwanted sexual activities. This can involve pressuring or forcing a partner to engage in sexual acts against their will, disregarding their boundaries, or engaging in non-consensual practices. Sexual exploitation can also occur when one partner uses sex as a transactional tool, demanding sexual acts in exchange for basic needs, such as food or shelter.

3. **Stigmatization and shame:** Abusers may use sexual abuse or assault to demean, degrade, or humiliate their partner. This can involve using derogatory language, engaging in acts that cause physical or emotional pain, or making a partner feel ashamed or guilty about their sexuality. By doing so, the abuser seeks to control the victim's self-esteem and reinforce their power over them.

4. **Barriers to seeking help:** Societal expectations, gender roles, and cultural norms can create barriers for victims of domestic violence to seek help or report the abuse. For example, men may face stigma, disbelief, or societal pressure to conform to traditional notions of masculinity, which can make it more challenging for them to disclose abuse, especially if it involves sexual violence. Additionally, societal attitudes and misconceptions about sex and consent can further complicate the reporting and understanding of sexual abuse within domestic violence situations.

5. **Economic dependence:** Financial or economic factors can also contribute to the power dynamics in abusive relationships. Economic dependence on an abusive partner can make it more challenging for victims to leave the abusive situation, including instances where sexual coercion or exploitation is present. The abuser may use economic control as a means to manipulate and maintain power over the victim.

It is important to approach domestic violence holistically, recognizing that it involves multiple forms of abuse, including physical, emotional, psychological, and financial abuse, in addition to sexual abuse. Addressing domestic violence requires a comprehensive approach that encompasses education, awareness, legal protection, support services, and societal change. It is crucial to promote healthy relationship dynamics, gender equality, consent education, and provide support for all individuals affected by domestic violence.

Chapter 5

B ringing old emotional baggage into new relationships can be challenging and potentially harmful if not addressed properly. When someone enters a new relationship without resolving past emotional wounds or seeking counseling, it can negatively impact their ability to form healthy, fulfilling connections.

Here are a few considerations and suggestions for handling this situation:

1. **Self-reflection:** Encourage the individual to reflect on their past relationships and identify any unresolved issues or patterns that may be affecting their current mindset. This self-awareness can be a crucial first step in addressing and overcoming emotional baggage.

2. **Seek counseling or therapy:** Suggest that the person consider seeking professional help, such as counseling or therapy. A trained therapist can provide guidance, support, and tools to help them navigate their past traumas and develop healthier coping mechanisms.

3. **Communication and honesty:** Encourage open and honest communication within the new relationship. The individual needs to express their emotional struggles and inform their partner about their past experiences. This helps establish trust and understanding while allowing both parties to work together in overcoming any challenges that may arise.

4. **Patience and understanding:** Remind the individual to be patient with themselves and their partner. Healing from past wounds takes time, and it's essential to approach the process with understanding and compassion. Encourage them to maintain realistic expectations and avoid placing undue pressure on themselves or their relationship.

5. **Practice self-care:** Encourage the individual to engage in self-care activities that promote emotional healing and well-being. This can include activities like exercise, meditation, journaling, or engaging in hobbies they enjoy. Taking care of themselves can contribute to their overall emotional resilience and ability to navigate the challenges that come with addressing old baggage.

Remember, the individual needs to take responsibility for their emotional well-being and actively work on resolving their past issues. A professional counselor or therapist can provide specific guidance based on their unique circumstances, helping them develop healthier relationship patterns and create a brighter future.

Chapter 6

For a woman entering a new relationship with unresolved emotional baggage, it's important to approach the situation with care and consideration. Here are some specific suggestions for her:

1. **Self-awareness:** Encourage the woman to reflect on her past relationship and identify any unresolved emotional wounds or patterns that may be impacting her current mindset. Developing self-awareness can help her better understand her feelings and behaviors in relationships.

2. **Seek counseling or therapy:** Suggest that she consider seeking professional help, such as counseling or therapy. A trained therapist can provide a safe space for her to explore her past experiences, process her emotions, and develop strategies for moving forward. Therapy can also assist her in developing healthier coping mechanisms and communication skills.

3. **Open communication with her partner:** Encourage open and honest communication between her and her new partner. She needs to express her emotional struggles and inform her partner about her past experiences. This creates an environment of trust and understanding, allowing both individuals to work together in supporting each other's healing process.

4. **Patience and understanding:** Remind her to be patient with herself and her partner. Healing from past wounds takes time, and it's important to approach the process with understanding and compassion. Encourage her to communicate her needs and boundaries while also being supportive of her partner's journey.

5. **Self-care and self-love:** Encourage her to prioritize self-care and self-love. This includes engaging in activities that promote emotional well-being, setting boundaries, practicing self-compassion, and surrounding herself with a supportive network of friends and loved ones. Taking care of herself will contribute to her overall healing and resilience.

It's important to note that healing from past relationship trauma is a personal journey, and everyone's process is unique. Encourage her to seek professional guidance to address her specific needs and challenges. With time, support, and self-reflection, she can work towards building healthier and happier relationships in the future.

Chapter 7

For a man who is carrying emotional baggage from a past relationship into a new one.

Here are some suggestions on how to cope and navigate the next relationship:

1. **Self-reflection and healing:** Take the time to reflect on the previous relationship and the emotions associated with it. Acknowledge and process any unresolved feelings, grief, or trauma. Consider seeking therapy or counseling to support your healing journey and gain insight into the patterns or triggers that may be affecting your current mindset.

2. **Set realistic expectations:** Recognize that every relationship is unique, and it's important not to project past hurts or assumptions onto your new partner. Be mindful of any negative thought patterns or limiting beliefs that may arise, and consciously challenge them. Remind yourself that your new partner is not responsible for the actions or mistakes of your past partner.

3. **Open communication:** Foster open and honest communication with your new partner. Share your experiences and concerns, making sure to express your needs, fears, and boundaries. Effective communication can help build trust and understanding, creating a solid foundation for the relationship.

4. **Patience and self-compassion:** Be patient with yourself and allow yourself time to heal. Understand that healing is a process, and it is normal to experience ups and downs along the way. Practice self-compassion and self-care, being kind to yourself as you navigate the new relationship.

5. **Focus on personal growth:** Use this opportunity to focus on personal growth and self-improvement. Engage in activities that promote self-esteem, self-confidence, and overall well-being. Pursue hobbies, interests, and goals that bring you joy and fulfillment outside of the relationship.

6. **Learn from the past:** Reflect on the lessons learned from your previous relationship. Identify any patterns or behaviors that contributed to the breakdown and actively work on improving yourself. Use the past as a learning experience to make better choices and create healthier dynamics in your new relationship.

Remember, building a healthy and fulfilling relationship takes time, effort, and mutual understanding. By taking care of your emotional well-being, communicating openly, and being mindful of your past experiences, you can increase your chances of creating a positive and mutually supportive partnership.

Chapter 8

D ealing with a person who is struggling with addiction, whether it's alcohol or drugs, can be challenging.

Here are some suggestions on how to approach the situation:

1. **Educate yourself:** Learn about addiction, its effects, and the available treatment options. Understanding addiction as a complex disease can help you approach the situation with empathy and knowledge.

2. **Encourage professional help:** Suggest that the person seek professional assistance, such as addiction counselors, therapists, or rehabilitation programs. Encourage them to explore treatment options that suit their needs and provide ongoing support.

3. **Express concern and support:** Let the person know that you are genuinely concerned about their well-being. Offer your support and express your willingness to help them seek treatment or connect them with appropriate resources. Be compassionate and non-judgmental in your approach, as addiction is a deeply personal struggle.

4. **Set boundaries:** Establish clear boundaries to protect yourself and your well-being. This may include setting limits on enabling behaviors, such as providing financial support or

covering up for their actions. Boundaries help create a healthier dynamic and encourage the person to take responsibility for their recovery.

5. **Encourage a support network:** Encourage the person to engage with support groups or communities, such as Alcoholics Anonymous (AA) or Narcotics Anonymous (NA). These groups provide a safe space for individuals to share their experiences, receive support, and connect with others who are going through similar struggles.

6. **Practice self-care:** Taking care of yourself is crucial when dealing with someone going through addiction. Seek support for yourself through therapy, support groups, or counseling. Ensure that you have a strong support system in place to help you navigate the challenges and emotions that may arise.

7. **Avoid enabling behaviors:** Refrain from enabling the person's addiction by providing them with substances, covering up their actions, or making excuses for their behavior. Enabling can perpetuate the cycle of addiction and hinder their recovery process.

8. **Practice patience and understanding:** Recovery from addiction is a challenging and ongoing process. Be patient with the person as they navigate their journey. Understand that setbacks and relapses may occur, and offer support and encouragement to get back on track.

It's important to remember that you cannot force someone to seek help or overcome addiction. Ultimately, the decision and commitment to recovery lie with the individual. Your role is to provide support, encouragement, and access to resources, but the person must take responsibility for their healing.

Chapter 9

Dealing with individuals who have experienced childhood abuse and are struggling to let go of the situation requires empathy, understanding, and a patient approach.

Here are some suggestions on how to support them:

1. **Encourage professional help:** Suggest that the person seek therapy or counseling from a qualified mental health professional experienced in trauma and abuse. They can provide the necessary tools and guidance to help the individual process their experiences, heal emotional wounds, and develop coping strategies.

2. **Be a supportive listener:** Create a safe and non-judgmental space for the person to express their feelings and thoughts. Encourage them to talk about their experiences, but respect their boundaries if they're not ready to share. Avoid pressuring them to disclose details before they're comfortable.

3. **Validate their emotions:** Acknowledge their pain, anger, and frustration without trying to dismiss or minimize their feelings. Let them know that their emotions are valid and that you're there to support them through their healing journey.

4. **Educate yourself:** Learn about the effects of childhood abuse, such as trauma responses, triggers, and coping mechanisms.

This knowledge will help you better understand what they're going through and how to respond appropriately.

5. **Encourage self-care:** Promote healthy self-care practices, such as exercise, proper nutrition, and sufficient rest. Encourage them to engage in activities they enjoy and find therapeutic, such as practicing mindfulness, journaling, or pursuing hobbies.

6. **Respect their boundaries:** Understand that healing is a personal process, and everyone progresses at their own pace. Respect their boundaries if they're not ready to discuss certain topics or engage in specific activities. Pushing them beyond their comfort zone may cause more harm than good.

7. **Offer practical support:** Help them find resources, such as support groups, books, or online communities, where they can connect with others who have had similar experiences. Offer to accompany them to therapy sessions or appointments, if they feel comfortable with it.

8. **Be patient and persistent:** Recovery from childhood abuse can be a long and challenging journey. It's important to be patient and persistent in your support, even if progress seems slow or setbacks occur. Remind them that healing is possible and that they're not alone.

Remember, it's crucial to prioritize the person's well-being and respect their autonomy. If you believe they're in immediate danger or at risk of self-harm, encourage them to contact a helpline or emergency services for professional intervention.

Chapter 10

I t's important to note that not all men feel the need to abuse or harm women, and it would be incorrect to generalize such behavior to all men. However, there are cases where some men engage in abusive or violent behavior towards women, and it is essential to understand the underlying factors that contribute to such actions.

Abuse and violence towards women stem from complex social, cultural, psychological, and individual factors.

Here are a few possible reasons why some men may engage in such behavior:

1. **Socialization and cultural norms:** Societal norms, stereotypes, and expectations can influence how men perceive their roles and power dynamics in relationships. Traditional gender roles that promote male dominance and control can contribute to a mindset where some men believe they have a right to exert power over women.

2. **Learned behavior:** Some individuals may grow up in environments where they witness or experience violence, which can normalize and perpetuate abusive behavior. This can include witnessing domestic violence in their own homes or being exposed to violent media.

3. **Power and control:** Abuse is often rooted in a desire for power and control over another person. Some individuals may feel threatened by women who challenge their power or independence, leading to abusive behavior as a way to exert control and maintain a sense of dominance.

4. **Psychological factors:** Certain individuals may have underlying psychological issues, such as personality disorders, unresolved trauma, or deep-seated anger and resentment, which can contribute to abusive behavior. However, it is important to note that having psychological issues does not justify or excuse abusive actions.

5. **Substance abuse:** Alcohol or drug abuse can impair judgment, lower inhibitions, and contribute to aggressive behavior. While substance abuse does not cause abuse directly, it can exacerbate existing tendencies or impair self-control, increasing the likelihood of violent actions.

It's crucial to emphasize that abusive behavior is not justified under any circumstances. Abusing or harming another individual is a violation of their rights and autonomy. Efforts should focus on promoting gender equality, challenging harmful stereotypes, educating individuals about healthy relationships, and holding offenders accountable through legal systems and support services.

Chapter 11

During the Jim Crow era in the United States, which lasted roughly from the late 19th century to the mid-20th century, African Americans faced systemic racial segregation and discrimination. The Jim Crow laws enforced racial segregation in public facilities, transportation, housing, education, and employment, effectively creating a separate and unequal society for African Americans.

The impact of Jim Crow on the African-American community was profound and multifaceted. Segregation and discriminatory practices limited economic opportunities, education, and political power for African Americans. It created significant social and economic disparities between African Americans and white Americans.

Regarding welfare and its impact on separating fathers from the home, it is important to note that the welfare system is complex and multifaceted, and its effects cannot be simplistically attributed to a single factor. Indeed, certain aspects of welfare policies implemented during and after the Jim Crow era had unintended consequences on family dynamics within the African-American community.

In the 1960's, as part of President Lyndon B. Johnson's Great Society initiatives, welfare programs such as Aid to Families with Dependent Children (**AFDC**) were expanded. These programs were designed to alleviate poverty and provide assistance to low-income families. However, certain eligibility criteria had unintended consequences on family structures.

At the time, **AFDC** and similar programs established that to qualify for benefits, the presence of a male breadwinner in the household was considered a disqualifying factor. This policy, known as the "man-in-the-house" rule, created a disincentive for African-American fathers to live with their families for the mother and children to receive welfare benefits. As a result, some families faced difficult choices between financial support and keeping the family together.

It is important to recognize that the "man-in-the-house" rule was not exclusive to African Americans, as it affected families of all races. However, due to the economic challenges faced by many African Americans as a result of historical and ongoing racial discrimination, the impact of such policies was disproportionately felt within their communities.

It is also worth noting that the separation of fathers from their families cannot be solely attributed to welfare policies. The legacy of slavery, systemic racism, economic disparities, and the broader social and cultural context of the time all played significant roles in shaping family dynamics within the African-American community.

Since the Jim Crow era and the implementation of welfare policies, significant changes have occurred in the United States. The **AFDC** program was replaced by Temporary Assistance for Needy Families (**TANF**) in 1996, which introduced work requirements and time limits. These changes aimed to promote self-sufficiency and discourage long-term dependence on welfare.

It is essential to approach the topic with nuance and avoid oversimplification. The impact of historical events, discriminatory practices, and social policies on the African-American community is complex and multifaceted, and it is important to consider a range of factors when discussing the effects of welfare and family structures during and after the Jim Crow era.

Chapter 12

The impact of divorce or breakups on children can be significant and varied. While every child and family situation is unique, research suggests that children may experience a range of emotional, social, and academic challenges during and after a divorce or breakup.

Here are some common effects:

1. **Emotional distress:** Children may experience a wide range of emotions such as sadness, anger, confusion, anxiety, and guilt. They may struggle with feelings of abandonment, loss, and insecurity.

2. **Behavioral changes:** Children may exhibit changes in behavior, including acting out, aggressiveness, withdrawal, or regression in younger children. They may also experience difficulties in school, such as decreased academic performance or problems with attention and concentration.

3. **Relationship difficulties:** Children may have difficulties forming and maintaining relationships, both with their parents and peers. They may develop trust issues and have concerns about future relationships and commitments.

4. **Self-esteem issues:** Children may blame themselves for the divorce or breakup, leading to lowered self-esteem and feelings

of guilt. They may question their worth and feel a sense of rejection.

5. **Stress and physical health problems:** The stress of divorce or breakup can impact a child's physical health, leading to problems such as headaches, stomachaches, sleep disturbances, and weakened immune systems.

It's important to note that not all children experience these effects, and some may display resilience and adapt well to the changes. The impact of divorce or breakup can also be influenced by various factors, including the child's age, temperament, level of parental conflict, and the presence of a strong support network.

To mitigate the negative impact, parents must prioritize their children's well-being and provide them with consistent, loving, and supportive environments. Open communication, reassurance, and involving children in the decision-making process when appropriate can help them cope with the changes more effectively. In some cases, seeking professional counseling or therapy can be beneficial for both children and parents to navigate the challenges associated with divorce or breakups.

Chapter 13

The impact of a woman who engages in mental, physical, and verbal abuse can be significant and far-reaching. Abuse in any form is a serious issue and can cause severe harm to the victim's physical and mental well-being.

Here are some potential impacts of such abuse:

1. **Physical Impact:** Physical abuse can lead to visible injuries such as bruises, broken bones, scars, and chronic pain. It may also result in long-term health problems, including physical disabilities. The victim may require medical intervention and treatment to recover from the physical harm caused by the abuse.

2. **Emotional and Psychological Impact:** Mental and verbal abuse can have profound emotional and psychological consequences. Victims may experience low self-esteem, depression, anxiety, and post-traumatic stress disorder (**PTSD**). They may develop a sense of helplessness, worthlessness, and hopelessness. The constant berating, insults, and degrading comments can erode their self-confidence and self-worth over time.

3. **Cognitive Impact:** Prolonged abuse can affect cognitive functioning. Victims may have difficulty concentrating, making decisions, and maintaining focus. They may experience memory problems and have trouble processing information. Chronic stress resulting from abuse can also impact the brain's ability to function optimally.

4. **Social Impact:** Abuse can isolate victims from their friends, family, and support networks. The abuser may control the victim's social interactions, limit their access to resources, and manipulate their relationships. This isolation can lead to feelings of loneliness, lack of social support, and difficulty in forming healthy relationships in the future.

5. **Interpersonal Impact:** Victims of abuse may find it challenging to establish trust and maintain healthy relationships. They may struggle with intimacy, have difficulty expressing emotions, and fear entering into new relationships due to the trauma they have experienced.

6. **Economic Impact:** In some cases, abuse can result in financial dependence on the abuser. The victim may be prevented from working or accessing financial resources, leaving them financially vulnerable and unable to support themselves or their children.

7. **Long-term Consequences:** The effects of abuse can be long-lasting. Even after escaping the abusive situation, survivors may continue to experience emotional and psychological difficulties. They may require ongoing therapy, support, and rehabilitation to recover fully and rebuild their lives.

It is important to note that the impact of abuse can vary from person to person, and not all individuals will experience the same effects. However, it is crucial to recognize the seriousness of abuse and provide support, resources, and interventions to help survivors heal and regain control over their lives.

Chapter 14

Experiencing abuse, whether it's mental, physical, or verbal, can have a significant impact on anyone, including men. Abuse is a harmful and traumatic experience that can affect a person's physical and mental well-being, as well as their overall quality of life.

Here are some potential impacts on a man who is experiencing abuse:

1. **Emotional and psychological effects:** Abuse can lead to various emotional and psychological effects, such as anxiety, depression, low self-esteem, and feelings of worthlessness. The constant belittlement, insults, and humiliation associated with verbal abuse can deeply affect a person's self-perception and emotional stability.

2. **Physical health consequences:** Physical abuse can result in physical injuries, ranging from minor bruises and cuts to more severe injuries like broken bones, concussions, or internal organ damage. The ongoing physical abuse can have long-term health consequences, including chronic pain, mobility issues, and increased vulnerability to future injuries.

3. **Isolation and social withdrawal:** Abused men may feel isolated and cut off from their support networks. Perpetrators of abuse often use manipulative tactics to control their victims, including isolating them from friends, family, and

social activities. This social withdrawal can further exacerbate feelings of loneliness, helplessness, and despair.

4. **Impact on relationships:** Abuse can strain relationships with friends, family members, and romantic partners. Victims of abuse may struggle to trust others, experience difficulties in forming new relationships, or have challenges maintaining healthy relationships due to the negative impact of abuse on their emotional well-being.

5. **Substance abuse and self-destructive behaviors:** Some individuals subjected to abuse may turn to substance abuse as a coping mechanism. Drugs, alcohol, or other self-destructive behaviors can temporarily numb emotional pain or provide an escape from the abusive situation. However, such behaviors can lead to additional health problems and further complicate the recovery process.

6. **Work and academic performance:** The effects of abuse can spill over into various areas of life, including work or academic performance. The trauma and emotional distress associated with abuse can make it difficult for a person to concentrate, perform well, or maintain employment or educational commitments.

It is important to note that every individual responds to abuse differently, and the impact can vary based on factors such as the severity and duration of the abuse, the presence of support systems, and individual resilience. If you or someone you know is experiencing abuse, it is crucial to seek help and support from trusted individuals, helplines, or professional organizations specializing in domestic violence or abuse.

Chapter 15

Showing love to someone who has never experienced it in their childhood can be a deeply meaningful and transformative experience for them. It requires patience, understanding, and a willingness to create a safe and nurturing environment.

Here are some suggestions on how to show love to such an individual:

1. **Be patient and understanding:** Recognize that their experiences may have shaped their perception of love and relationships. Be patient with their emotional barriers and understand that it may take time for them to trust and accept love.

2. **Create a safe and supportive environment:** Foster a safe and nurturing environment where they feel comfortable expressing their thoughts, emotions, and vulnerabilities. Encourage open communication and assure them that their feelings are valid and respected.

3. **Show consistent affection:** Express your love and care through both words and actions. Offer hugs, hand-holding, or other physical gestures of affection, if they are comfortable with it. Consistency is key to building trust and security.

4. **Listen actively:** Give them your undivided attention and actively listen when they want to share their thoughts and

feelings. Validate their experiences and provide empathy and support without judgment.

5. **Practice empathy:** Try to understand their unique perspective and experiences. Put yourself in their shoes and acknowledge the impact their past has had on their ability to give and receive love. This will help you respond to their needs with greater sensitivity.

6. **Be supportive and encouraging:** Encourage their personal growth and be supportive of their endeavors. Celebrate their achievements and provide reassurance during challenging times. Offer words of affirmation to boost their self-esteem and let them know that you believe in their abilities.

7. **Be a consistent presence:** Show up consistently in their life and be reliable. This will help build trust and demonstrate that your love is enduring and steadfast.

8. **Seek professional help if needed:** If the person has deep emotional wounds or trauma from their childhood, consider encouraging them to seek professional help from therapists or counselors who specialize in trauma and attachment issues. Professional guidance can be instrumental in their healing process.

Remember, everyone's journey is unique, and the process of healing and learning to accept love takes time. Be patient, understanding, and compassionate throughout the journey, and always respect their boundaries and individual needs.

Chapter 16

I nsecurities and animosity in a relationship in the beginning and not sure if you trust your partner.

Insecurities and animosity in the beginning of a relationship can be challenging and can create a sense of uncertainty and doubt. Trust is an essential foundation for any healthy relationship, and it takes time to build.

If you're feeling insecure and unsure about trusting your partner, here are a few suggestions:

1. **Self-reflection**: Take some time to reflect on your own insecurities and concerns. Ask yourself if they are rooted in past experiences or are specific to this relationship. Understanding your own triggers can help you address them more effectively.

2. **Open communication**: Talk openly and honestly with your partner about your concerns and insecurities. Share your feelings and fears, and encourage them to do the same. Having open conversations can foster understanding and help build trust.

3. **Time and patience**: Building trust takes time. Allow the relationship to develop naturally and give yourself and your partner space and time to get to know each other better. As you spend more time together and see consistent positive actions, your trust in your partner may grow.

4. **Observe their actions**: Pay attention to your partner's actions and behavior. Trust is built on consistency and reliability. Look for signs that they are trustworthy, such as keeping their promises, being there for you when you need support, and showing respect and honesty.

5. **Set healthy boundaries**: Establishing and maintaining healthy boundaries is crucial. Clearly communicate your needs and expectations to your partner, and ensure they do the same. Respect for each other's boundaries can help create a sense of security in the relationship.

6. **Seek support if needed**: If your insecurities and trust issues persist and significantly impact your well-being or the relationship, consider seeking support from a therapist or counselor. They can provide guidance, help you explore your feelings, and offer strategies to build trust and address any underlying issues.

Remember, building trust is a gradual process, and it requires effort and commitment from both partners. It's essential to be patient with yourself and your partner as you navigate through these challenges together.

Chapter 17

How to show love to a man or a woman that is broken.

Showing love and support to someone who is mentally broken can be a deeply compassionate and meaningful gesture.

Here are some suggestions on how to show love to a person who is struggling mentally, regardless of their gender:

1. **Be a good listener:** Create a safe and non-judgmental space for them to express their thoughts and feelings. Practice active listening by giving them your full attention, maintaining eye contact, and responding with empathy.

2. **Offer your presence:** Simply being there for them can make a significant difference. Spend quality time together, engage in activities they enjoy, or simply be a comforting presence by sitting together quietly.

3. **Practice empathy and understanding:** Try to put yourself in their shoes and understand their perspective. Validate their emotions and let them know that you understand and care about what they're going through.

4. **Be patient and non-judgmental:** Recovery from mental health challenges takes time. Avoid pressuring them to "get over it" or "snap out of it." Instead, be patient, supportive, and understanding of their journey.

5. **Educate yourself about their condition:** Learn about their mental health condition or the challenges they are facing. Understanding their struggles can help you empathize better and provide more effective support.

6. **Encourage professional help:** Suggest that they seek professional help from therapists, counselors, or mental health specialists. Offer to assist them in finding appropriate resources or accompany them to appointments if they're comfortable with it.

7. **Offer practical support:** Help them with day-to-day tasks or responsibilities when needed. This could include cooking a meal, running errands, or assisting with household chores. Small acts of kindness can alleviate some of their stress and show your support.

8. **Express your love and appreciation:** Let them know that you care for them deeply. Offer words of encouragement, appreciation, and love. Remind them of their strengths and the positive qualities you see in them.

9. **Respect their boundaries:** Understand that everyone has different comfort levels when it comes to receiving help and support. Respect their boundaries and give them the space they need when necessary.

10. **Encourage self-care:** Support and encourage them to prioritize self-care activities that promote their well-being. This could include exercise, engaging in hobbies, practicing mindfulness, or seeking out activities that bring them joy.

Remember, it's important to take care of yourself as well while supporting someone who is mentally broken. Reach out to your support network and seek guidance from professionals if needed.

Chapter 18

D ealing with a narcissistic partner.
Dealing with a narcissistic partner in a domestic violent relationship?
dealing with a narcissistic partner in a domestic violent relationship. Narcissistic individuals can be challenging to deal with, especially in a situation as serious as domestic violence.

Here are some general suggestions for managing this difficult situation:

1. **Prioritize your safety:** Your safety is the most important thing. If you're in immediate danger, reach out to local law enforcement or a domestic violence hotline in your country. They can provide you with the necessary support and resources.

2. **Seek professional help:** Consider reaching out to a therapist or counselor who specializes in domestic violence and narcissistic abuse. They can help you navigate the complex dynamics of the relationship, provide emotional support, and develop a safety plan.

3. **Build a support network:** Reach out to friends, family members, or support groups that can offer you emotional support and understanding. Connecting with others who have experienced similar situations can be empowering and help you feel less alone.

4. **Document incidents:** Keep a record of any abusive incidents, including dates, times, and descriptions of what happened. This documentation can serve as evidence if you decide to involve the authorities or seek legal protection.

5. **Establish boundaries:** Set clear boundaries with your partner and communicate your needs assertively. However, be aware that narcissistic individuals may not respect boundaries, so it's crucial to prioritize your safety.

6. **Develop an exit plan:** If you're considering leaving the relationship, it's important to have a plan in place. This may involve seeking legal advice, gathering important documents, securing a safe place to stay, and accessing financial resources.

7. **Practice self-care:** Take care of your physical and emotional well-being. Engage in activities that bring you joy and provide stress relief. Consider mindfulness exercises, regular exercise, and seeking activities that promote your overall well-being.

Remember, every situation is unique, and it's important to consult with professionals who can provide personalized advice based on your specific circumstances. Domestic violence hotlines, counseling services, and local support groups can offer additional guidance and resources.

Chapter 19

Trying to deal with an alpha male or female in a relationship?

Dealing with someone who exhibits alpha traits in a relationship can sometimes be challenging, as such individuals tend to be dominant, assertive, and strong-willed. However, it's important to remember that every individual is unique, and it's not solely defined by their gender.

Here are some general tips for navigating a relationship with someone who displays alpha characteristics:

1. **Communication:** Open and honest communication is crucial in any relationship. Clearly express your thoughts, feelings, and expectations, and encourage your partner to do the same. Effective communication can help establish boundaries, resolve conflicts, and foster understanding between both parties.

2. **Mutual respect:** It's essential to maintain respect for each other's opinions, feelings, and needs. Avoid belittling or undermining your partner's thoughts or actions. Likewise, expect the same level of respect in return.

3. **Equality:** Focus on establishing a relationship that is based on equality and collaboration rather than dominance and submission. Encourage shared decision-making, compromise, and cooperation in various aspects of your relationship.

4. **Set boundaries:** Clearly define personal boundaries and expectations within the relationship. Discuss what is acceptable and unacceptable behavior for both parties. This can help prevent any feelings of being dominated or controlled.

5. **Maintain independence:** It's important for each individual to maintain their own sense of identity and independence within the relationship. Encourage your partner to pursue their interests, and make sure you have time for your own personal growth as well.

6. **Find common ground:** Discover shared interests and activities that you both enjoy. Engaging in these activities together can help foster a sense of unity and strengthen your bond.

7. **Seek compromise:** Alpha individuals often have strong opinions and can be assertive about their desires. It's important to find a balance between asserting your own needs and finding compromise with your partner. Look for win-win solutions that satisfy both parties.

8. **Support and encouragement:** Offer support and encouragement to your partner's ambitions and goals. Appreciate their strengths and achievements, and let them know that you're there to support them.

Remember, every relationship is unique, and these tips may not apply to every situation. It's crucial to understand and adapt to your partner's specific personality traits, needs, and communication style.

Chapter 20

Here is to deal with relationship with regards to sex only and not personal attributes?

When approaching a relationship with a focus solely on sex and without considering personal attributes, it is important to recognize and respect the boundaries and expectations of both parties involved.

Here are some guidelines to consider:

1. **Communication:** Have an open and honest conversation with your partner about your intentions, desires, and expectations. Clearly discuss the nature of the relationship, ensuring that both parties are on the same page and have consented to engage in a purely sexual relationship.

2. **Boundaries:** Establish boundaries and limits that are comfortable for both individuals. Discuss what you are comfortable with and what you are not willing to engage in. Consent should always be enthusiastic, ongoing, and mutual.

3. **Emotional detachment:** Understand that in a relationship focused solely on sex, emotional attachment may be limited or absent. Be prepared to maintain emotional distance and avoid developing strong feelings for your partner.

4. **Respect and honesty:** Treat your partner with respect and honesty. Be transparent about your intentions and make sure to address any concerns or issues that arise during the course of the relationship.

5. **Safety and protection:** Prioritize sexual health and safety. Practice safe sex by using condoms or other forms of contraception, and consider regular testing for sexually transmitted infections (**STIs**).

6. **Regular communication:** Continually check in with your partner to ensure that both parties remain satisfied with the arrangement. If either person begins to develop deeper feelings or desires a change in the nature of the relationship, it is crucial to communicate these feelings openly and honestly.

Remember, it is essential to approach any relationship, regardless of its nature, with honesty, respect, and consideration for the feelings and well-being of both individuals involved.

Chapter 21

How important is celibacy before relationship?

The reason why I ask the question is because I've been in several relationships in my life and I've came to the conclusion that's what I want it to do thus far I've been celibate almost 4 years now and it's been the happiest for years of my life my personal opinion no... because I was broken and I needed to fix myself and I'm still in the process of doing that.

The importance of celibacy before entering a relationship varies depending on personal beliefs, values, and cultural or religious considerations. Celibacy refers to abstaining from sexual activity, and some individuals may choose to practice it for various reasons.

For some people, celibacy before a relationship may be important due to religious or spiritual beliefs. In certain religious traditions, celibacy is seen as a way to maintain purity, focus on spiritual growth, or adhere to specific teachings or practices. In such cases, individuals may choose to abstain from sexual activity until they are ready to commit to a long-term relationship, such as marriage.

Additionally, celibacy can be a personal choice based on individual values, priorities, or life circumstances. Some people may choose celibacy as a means of personal growth, self-discovery, or emotional well-being. They might want to establish a strong foundation for a future relationship by focusing on personal development, career goals, or other areas of life without the distractions and complications that can arise from sexual relationships.

On the other hand, celibacy is not a universal requirement or expectation before entering a relationship. Many people choose to engage in consensual sexual relationships before committing to a long-term partnership. Sexual intimacy can be an important aspect of romantic relationships for many individuals, and exploring compatibility in this area can be considered important.

Ultimately, the importance of celibacy before a relationship is a personal decision that varies from individual to individual. It is essential to have open and honest communication with potential partners about personal values, expectations, and boundaries regarding sexual activity to ensure compatibility and mutual understanding.

Chapter 22

Love and trust in a relationship where regards to send that you love someone but not trusting them?

Love and trust are both important components of a healthy and fulfilling relationship. While it is possible to love someone and not fully trust them, it can create challenges and potential issues within the relationship.

Trust forms the foundation of a strong and lasting relationship. It involves having confidence in your partner's integrity, actions, and intentions. Without trust, doubts, suspicion, and insecurity can arise, leading to misunderstandings, conflicts, and emotional distress.

When you love someone but struggle to trust them, it's important to explore the reasons behind your lack of trust. Has your partner done something to break your trust in the past, or is it a result of your own personal insecurities or past experiences? Identifying the root causes can help you address the issue more effectively.

Communication is crucial in these situations. Openly discuss your concerns and fears with your partner, expressing your need for trust and understanding. It's essential to have honest conversations about your expectations, boundaries, and what actions could help build trust over time.

Building trust takes effort from both partners. The person who has broken trust must be willing to make amends, be transparent, and demonstrate through their actions that they are trustworthy. The other person must be open to forgiving and giving their partner an opportunity to rebuild trust.

However, it's also important to recognize that trust cannot be forced or demanded. It takes time and consistent positive experiences to rebuild trust. Both partners need to be patient, supportive, and willing to work through the challenges together.

If the lack of trust persists despite efforts to address it, it may be necessary to seek professional help, such as couples' therapy. A trained therapist can provide guidance, help facilitate communication, and offer strategies to rebuild trust and strengthen the relationship.

Ultimately, love and trust go hand in hand. While it's possible to love someone without fully trusting them, it can create significant challenges and hinder the growth of the relationship. Open communication, understanding, and a willingness to work on the issue together are essential for rebuilding trust and nurturing a healthy, loving partnership.

Chapter 23

One of the biggest problems in relationships is insecurities how to handle insecurities in a relationship?

Handling insecurities in a relationship is crucial for maintaining a healthy and fulfilling partnership.

Here are some strategies that can help address and manage insecurities:

1. **Open and honest communication:** Talk to your partner about your insecurities and concerns. Share your feelings openly and calmly, expressing your needs and seeking reassurance. Effective communication can foster understanding and strengthen the bond between you.

2. **Self-reflection:** Take the time to reflect on the root causes of your insecurities. Understanding where they come from can help you address them more effectively. Consider if there are any past experiences or personal issues that contribute to your feelings of insecurity.

3. **Build self-esteem:** Work on improving your self-esteem and self-worth. Engage in activities that make you feel confident and accomplished. Surround yourself with supportive friends and engage in self-care practices that promote self-love and self-acceptance.

4. **Address trust issues:** Insecurities often stem from trust issues. If trust has been broken in the past, it may take time to rebuild it. Both partners should be committed to rebuilding trust through transparency, consistency, and keeping promises. Seek professional help if trust issues persist.

5. **Avoid comparisons:** Resist the temptation to compare yourself or your relationship to others. Remember that every relationship is unique, and focusing on comparisons only undermines your own happiness and satisfaction.

6. **Seek reassurance within the relationship:** Instead of seeking constant validation from external sources, work on building trust and seeking reassurance from your partner. Develop a sense of security by focusing on the love, support, and positive aspects of your relationship.

7. **Develop individual identities:** Nurture your individuality within the relationship. Pursue your own goals, interests, and hobbies. By maintaining a sense of self, you can reduce dependency on your partner for validation.

8. **Seek professional help if needed:** If your insecurities persist and significantly impact your relationship and overall well-being, consider seeking guidance from a therapist or counselor. They can provide you with valuable insights and strategies to address and manage your insecurities effectively.

Remember, addressing insecurities is a process that requires time, effort, and commitment from both partners. It's essential to create a supportive and understanding environment where both individuals can grow and heal together.

Chapter 24

H ow to handle relationships trying to deal with childhood abuse.

If experienced childhood abuse. Dealing with the effects of such trauma can be challenging, and it's important to approach relationships with sensitivity and care.

Here are some suggestions on how to handle relationships while trying to cope with childhood abuse:

1. **Seek therapy:** Consider working with a therapist or counselor who specializes in trauma and abuse. They can provide you with the necessary tools and support to navigate the challenges that may arise in relationships.

2. **Prioritize self-care:** Make self-care a priority in your life. Engage in activities that bring you joy, reduce stress, and promote your overall well-being. This may include exercising, practicing mindfulness or meditation, pursuing hobbies, or spending time with supportive friends and family.

3. **Communicate your needs:** Open and honest communication is vital in any relationship. Be open with your partner or loved ones about your experiences and how they may impact your behavior and emotions. Let them know what you need from them in terms of support and understanding.

4. **Set boundaries:** Establish clear boundaries to protect your emotional and physical well-being. Communicate your boundaries to your partner, and don't hesitate to enforce them if they are crossed. Boundaries help establish a sense of safety and control in your relationships.

5. **Practice self-compassion:** Be patient and kind to yourself as you navigate the healing process. Understand that healing takes time and it's okay to have ups and downs along the way. Treat yourself with the same compassion and understanding you would offer to a close friend.

6. **Educate yourself and your partner:** Learn about the effects of childhood abuse and trauma to gain a better understanding of your own experiences. Share this knowledge with your partner to help them better understand what you're going through. This can foster empathy and support within the relationship.

7. **Join support groups:** Consider joining support groups or online communities where you can connect with others who have experienced similar traumas. Sharing your experiences and listening to the stories of others can provide validation, support, and a sense of belonging.

Remember, healing from childhood abuse is a personal journey, and it's important to be patient with yourself. Surround yourself with understanding and supportive individuals who can help you through the process.

Chapter 25

H ow important relationships between the man and the woman can be so hard to deal with?

Relationships between men and women can be complex and challenging for a variety of reasons.

Here are a few factors that can contribute to the difficulties involved in such relationships:

1. **Differences in Communication Styles:** Men and women often have different ways of expressing themselves and communicating their thoughts and emotions. These differences can lead to misunderstandings, misinterpretations, and conflicts.

2. **Societal Expectations and Gender Roles:** Society often imposes certain expectations and roles on men and women, which can create pressure and strain in relationships. These societal norms, such as traditional gender roles, can influence behavior, responsibilities, and expectations within a relationship.

3. **Emotional Differences:** Men and women may have different emotional needs and ways of processing emotions. Women are often viewed as more emotionally expressive, while men may be socialized to be stoic and hide their emotions. These differences can lead to difficulties in understanding and supporting each other emotionally.

4. **Personal Differences:** Every individual has their own unique personality, experiences, values, and beliefs. These differences can create challenges in a relationship as individuals navigate their varying needs, desires, and perspectives.

5. **Lack of Effective Communication:** Communication is key in any relationship. However, effective communication requires active listening, empathy, and the ability to express oneself clearly. When couples struggle to communicate effectively, it can lead to misunderstandings, resentment, and unresolved conflicts.

6. **Unrealistic Expectations:** Sometimes, individuals enter into relationships with unrealistic expectations. They may expect their partner to fulfill all their needs and desires, or they may have unrealistic ideas about romance and love. Unrealistic expectations can put strain on a relationship and lead to disappointment.

7. **Past Baggage and Trauma:** Past experiences, such as previous failed relationships or traumatic events, can affect how individuals' approach and navigate new relationships. Unresolved emotional baggage and trauma can impact trust, intimacy, and overall relationship dynamics.

It's important to remember that while relationships can be challenging, they can also be incredibly fulfilling and rewarding. Open and honest communication, empathy, understanding, and a willingness to work through difficulties together can help couples navigate these challenges and foster a healthy, loving relationship.

Chapter 26

T he importance of a healthy relationship consists of

A healthy relationship is characterized by various important factors that contribute to its overall well-being.

Here are some key aspects that highlight the importance of a healthy relationship:

1. **Effective Communication:** Open and honest communication is vital in any relationship. It allows partners to express their needs, concerns, and feelings, while also promoting understanding, empathy, and conflict resolution.

2. **Trust and Honesty:** Trust serves as the foundation of a healthy relationship. Trusting one another creates a sense of security, emotional safety, and reliability. Honesty, integrity, and keeping one's promises are essential for building and maintaining trust.

3. **Mutual Respect:** Respect is crucial for maintaining a healthy dynamic. Partners should value each other's opinions, boundaries, and autonomy. They should treat each other with kindness, consideration, and appreciation.

4. **Emotional Support:** A healthy relationship provides emotional support to each partner. It involves offering comfort, understanding, and encouragement during both good times

and challenging situations. Partners should be able to rely on each other for emotional stability and validation.

5. **Equality and Fairness:** Equality in a relationship means that both partners have equal rights, responsibilities, and decision-making power. Fairness involves treating each other justly and considering each other's needs and wants.

6. **Independence and Interdependence:** In a healthy relationship, each partner maintains their individuality while also fostering a sense of togetherness. It's important to have separate interests, hobbies, and personal space, as well as shared activities and goals.

7. **Conflict Resolution:** Disagreements and conflicts are inevitable in any relationship. However, the ability to resolve conflicts in a respectful and constructive manner is crucial. Healthy relationships involve active listening, compromise, and finding solutions that satisfy both partners.

8. **Quality Time and Intimacy:** Spending quality time together and maintaining a healthy level of intimacy are essential for building and strengthening the bond between partners. This includes engaging in activities, conversations, and gestures that foster emotional and physical connection.

9. **Shared Values and Goals:** Partners in a healthy relationship often share common values, beliefs, and long-term goals. This alignment creates a sense of unity and supports the growth and development of the relationship.

10. **Adaptability and Growth:** Healthy relationships are flexible and adaptable to the changes and challenges that life brings. Partners should be willing to grow individually and as a couple, accommodating personal and relationship development.

Overall, a healthy relationship requires continuous effort, commitment, and nurturing. It promotes happiness, well-being, and personal growth for both partners involved.

Chapter 27

How importance is having a healthy relationship between a man and a woman and their relationship towards their children

Yes, having a healthy relationship between a man and a woman, as well as their relationship with their children, is indeed very important. A healthy and nurturing family environment provides numerous benefits for the well-being and development of all family members.

Firstly, a healthy relationship between parents serves as a positive role model for their children. Children learn by observing their parents' interactions and behaviors, and they often emulate what they see. When parents demonstrate respect, love, and effective communication in their relationship, children are more likely to develop similar skills and behaviors in their own relationships as they grow older.

Secondly, a strong relationship between parents provides stability and emotional security for children. When parents maintain a loving and supportive partnership, children feel safe and secure within their family unit. This stability allows children to thrive emotionally, intellectually, and socially, as they have a solid foundation from which to explore the world.

Additionally, a healthy parental relationship fosters effective co-parenting. When parents have a positive relationship, they can work together as a team to raise their children. This involves making joint decisions, setting consistent boundaries, and providing a united front in parenting approaches. Effective co-parenting contributes to a harmonious and structured environment, which promotes the healthy development of children.

Moreover, a healthy relationship between parents enhances the overall well-being of the family. When parents prioritize their relationship and take care of their own emotional and physical needs, they are better equipped to meet the needs of their children. A strong partnership allows parents to balance their roles and responsibilities, reducing stress and promoting overall family happiness.

However, it's important to note that a healthy family dynamic is not limited to a traditional man-woman relationship. Families come in various forms, and the principles of love, respect, effective communication, and co-parenting apply regardless of gender or sexual orientation.

In conclusion, fostering a healthy relationship between parents, regardless of their gender, and nurturing a positive relationship with their children is crucial for the well-being and development of everyone involved. A healthy family dynamic provides stability, emotional security, positive role modeling, effective co-parenting, and overall happiness for all family members.

Chapter 28

H ow does a man or woman deal with a relationship that's either confusing or they just don't know how?

Dealing with a confusing or uncertain relationship can be challenging, but there are several steps that both men and women can take to navigate such situations.

Here are some suggestions:

1. **Reflect on your feelings:** Take some time to understand your own emotions and thoughts about the relationship. Consider what you want and need from a partner, and whether the current situation aligns with your expectations.

2. **Communicate openly:** Honest and open communication is crucial in any relationship. Express your concerns, doubts, and confusion with your partner in a calm and non-confrontational manner. Share your feelings and ask for their perspective on the situation. Effective communication can help bring clarity and understanding.

3. **Seek clarity:** If you're feeling confused, it's important to seek clarity about the relationship. Ask questions to gain a better understanding of your partner's intentions, goals, and expectations. Discuss whether you both are on the same page or have different visions for the relationship.

4. **Give it time:** Relationships can be complex, and it may take time to gain clarity. Avoid rushing into decisions or making assumptions prematurely. Allow space for the relationship to evolve and for both of you to gain a better understanding of your feelings and needs.

5. **Trust your instincts:** Pay attention to your gut feelings and intuition. If something feels off or consistently causes confusion, it's essential to trust your instincts. Your emotional well-being and happiness should be a priority, so don't ignore any red flags or persistent doubts.

6. **Seek support:** Reach out to your friends, family, or a trusted confidant for advice and support. Sometimes an outside perspective can provide valuable insights and help you gain clarity.

7. **Set boundaries:** Establish boundaries that protect your emotional well-being. If the confusion or uncertainty persists and starts to take a toll on your mental health, consider taking a step back or creating some space to evaluate the relationship objectively.

8. **Prioritize self-care:** Focus on self-care activities that help you maintain balance and emotional well-being. Engage in hobbies, exercise, spend time with loved ones, and practice self-reflection. Taking care of yourself will provide you with the strength and clarity to make decisions about the relationship.

Remember, every relationship is unique, and there's no one-size-fits-all solution. It's important to evaluate your own feelings and needs and make choices that align with your long-term happiness and well-being.

Chapter 29

How to deal with relationships man or a woman that you were never shown as a child with regards to physical or verbal acknowledgment

Dealing with relationships when you were never shown physical or verbal acknowledgment as a child can be challenging, but it's important to remember that you have the power to develop healthy relationships despite your past experiences.

Here are some suggestions to help you navigate these situations:

1. **Self-reflection:** Take time to reflect on how your upbringing has influenced your perception of relationships and acknowledgment. Understand that your past experiences may impact your behavior and expectations in relationships. Recognizing these patterns is the first step towards change.

2. **Communication:** Open and honest communication is crucial in any relationship. Express your needs, concerns, and emotions to your partner. Let them know how important acknowledgment is to you and how your childhood experiences have shaped your expectations.

3. **Therapy or counseling:** Consider seeking professional help from a therapist or counselor. They can provide guidance and support as you navigate your past experiences and their

impact on your current relationships. Therapy can help you develop healthy coping mechanisms, improve communication skills, and build self-esteem.

4. **Self-care and self-worth:** Focus on self-care and building a strong sense of self-worth. Engage in activities that bring you joy, practice self-compassion, and surround yourself with positive influences. Developing a healthy relationship with yourself will positively impact your relationships with others.

5. **Set boundaries:** Establishing and maintaining boundaries is essential for healthy relationships. Clearly communicate your boundaries to your partner and ensure they respect them. This includes boundaries around acknowledgment, physical touch, and communication.

6. **Patience and understanding:** Recognize that your partner may not fully understand the impact of your past experiences. Be patient and provide them with the opportunity to learn and grow alongside you. It takes time for both partners to adapt and find new ways of relating to each other.

7. **Seek support:** Reach out to supportive friends, family members, or support groups who can provide empathy, advice, and understanding. Connecting with others who have had similar experiences can be helpful and reassuring.

Remember, each relationship is unique, and it will take time and effort to develop new patterns and behaviors. Be patient with yourself and your partner as you navigate these challenges together.

Chapter 30

How to understand physical emotional And verbal abuse when you're not used to it.

Understanding and recognizing physical, emotional, and verbal abuse can be challenging, especially if you're not accustomed to it. However, it's important to be aware of the signs and patterns of abusive behavior to protect yourself or others from harm.

Here are some steps to help you understand and recognize abuse:

1. **Educate yourself:** Learn about the different forms of abuse, their signs, and their effects. There are numerous resources available online, such as articles, books, and helpline websites, that can provide valuable information.

2. **Identify the signs:** Abuse can manifest in various ways. Physical abuse involves physical harm, such as hitting, pushing, or restraining. Emotional abuse includes manipulation, humiliation, intimidation, or constant criticism. Verbal abuse involves using derogatory language, threats, or yelling to demean and control someone. Look for patterns of behavior that consistently make you feel fearful, anxious, or belittled.

3. **Trust your instincts:** If something doesn't feel right or makes you uncomfortable, trust your gut. Your feelings and emotions are valid, and it's essential to acknowledge and validate them.

4. **Seek support:** Talk to someone you trust about your concerns, such as a close friend, family member, or counselor. They can offer you guidance, support, and an outside perspective on the situation.

5. **Document incidents:** Keep a record of abusive incidents, including dates, times, descriptions, and any witnesses. This documentation can be helpful if you decide to involve authorities or seek legal action in the future.

6. **Reach out for professional help:** If you believe you're experiencing abuse, consider seeking professional help from a therapist, counselor, or helpline. They can provide guidance, support, and resources to help you navigate the situation.

7. **Establish boundaries:** Set clear boundaries with the abuser and communicate your limits. If they continue to violate these boundaries, it may be necessary to distance yourself from the person or seek legal intervention.

8. **Safety first:** If you're in immediate danger or feel unsafe, prioritize your safety above all else. Remove yourself from the abusive situation and seek help from the authorities or a local domestic violence shelter.

Remember, understanding and recognizing abuse is the first step towards breaking free from it. It's essential to prioritize your well-being and seek the support you need to protect yourself.

Chapter 31

A s a child when I experienced physical and verbal abuse I used to think if I went to sleep and I woke up everything will be better but when I woke up it was still the same and even now as an adult is still bothers me. How should I cope with that?

Childhood trauma can have a lasting impact, and it's understandable that it still bothered one as an adult. Coping with the effects of abuse can be a challenging and ongoing process, but there are steps you can take to help yourself heal.

Here are some suggestions:

1. **Seek professional help:** Consider finding a therapist or counselor who specializes in trauma and abuse. They can provide you with the necessary support, guidance, and tools to work through your past experiences and develop healthier coping mechanisms.

2. **Join a support group:** Connecting with others who have experienced similar traumas can be very helpful. Support groups offer a safe space to share your feelings, learn from others, and realize that you are not alone. Look for local support groups or online communities that focus on healing from abuse.

3. **Practice self-care:** Engage in activities that promote self-care and self-compassion. This could include engaging in hobbies you enjoy, taking time for relaxation and self-reflection, practicing

mindfulness or meditation, or engaging in physical exercise. Taking care of your physical and emotional well-being is essential.

4. **Educate yourself:** Learn about the effects of trauma and abuse to better understand your own experiences. Knowledge can empower you and help you make sense of your feelings and behaviors. There are many books, articles, and online resources available on the topic.

5. **Develop healthy coping mechanisms:** Identify healthy coping mechanisms that work for you. These could include journaling, expressing yourself through art or music, engaging in outdoor activities, or practicing deep breathing exercises. Experiment with different strategies and find what helps you manage stress and process your emotions in a healthy way.

6. **Build a support network:** Surround yourself with supportive and caring individuals. Share your experiences with trusted friends or family members who can provide a listening ear and offer emotional support. Building a strong support network can make a significant difference in your healing journey.

7. **Be patient with yourself:** Healing from trauma takes time, and everyone's journey is different. Be patient and kind to yourself as you navigate through the healing process. Allow yourself to feel and process your emotions, and remember that healing is a gradual process.

If you are struggling with the effects of abuse and find it difficult to cope, I strongly encourage you to reach out to a mental health professional. They can provide personalized guidance and support based on your specific needs and circumstances.

Chapter 32

I s there something wrong if you decide not to be in relationships anymore in regards to pass relationships,

Deciding not to be in relationships anymore is a personal choice, and there is usually nothing inherently wrong with it. People have different preferences and priorities when it comes to their personal lives, and it's important to respect and honor those choices.

If you have decided not to be in relationships anymore, it could be for various reasons. Perhaps you have had negative experiences in past relationships that have caused you to reevaluate your priorities or emotional well-being. Maybe you have other goals or commitments that you want to focus on, such as personal development, career aspirations, or self-discovery.

It's essential to reflect on your reasons and ensure that you are making a decision that aligns with your values, needs, and long-term happiness. If you find that not being in relationships anymore brings you peace, contentment, and personal growth, then it can be a healthy choice for you.

However, it's worth noting that human emotions and desires can change over time. While you might feel content with your decision now, it's possible that your feelings might evolve in the future. Keep an open mind and be willing to reassess your choices as you continue to grow and learn more about yourself.

Ultimately, the most important thing is to prioritize your own well-being and do what feels right for you. It's okay to choose a path that deviates from societal expectations or other people's opinions as long as it brings you fulfillment and happiness.

Chapter 33

Attitude and communicating in relationships where regards to trying to get your point across

When it comes to trying to get your point across in a relationship, it's important to approach the situation with the right attitude and effective communication strategies.

Here are some tips to consider:

1. **Choose the right time and place:** Find a suitable time when both you and your partner are open and receptive to discussing important matters. Avoid bringing up sensitive topics in the heat of the moment or in public settings where privacy may be compromised.

2. **Be calm and composed:** Keep your emotions in check and approach the conversation with a calm demeanor. Being overly aggressive, defensive, or confrontational can escalate tensions and hinder effective communication.

3. **Practice active listening:** Give your partner your full attention and actively listen to their perspective without interrupting. Show empathy and try to understand their point of view before presenting your own.

4. **Use "I" statements:** Frame your thoughts and concerns using "I" statements rather than "you" statements. For example, say

"I feel" or "I think" instead of "You always" or "You never." This helps to avoid sounding accusatory and allows you to express your emotions or thoughts without placing blame.

5. **Be specific and clear:** Clearly articulate your point of view, providing specific examples or instances to support your argument. Vague or general statements can lead to confusion and misinterpretation.

6. **Avoid personal attacks:** Focus on the issue at hand rather than attacking your partner personally. Stick to discussing behaviors, actions, or situations, and avoid making sweeping generalizations or derogatory remarks.

7. **Seek mutual understanding:** Aim for a mutual understanding and compromise. Be open to hearing your partner's perspective and finding a middle ground that satisfies both parties. Remember that relationships are about teamwork and finding solutions together.

8. **Stay respectful:** Treat your partner with respect, even if you disagree with their viewpoint. Avoid derogatory language, insults, or belittling comments. Instead, foster a safe and respectful environment for open communication.

9. **Be patient and flexible:** Recognize that effective communication takes time and effort. It may require multiple conversations to fully understand each other's viewpoints and find common ground. Be patient, open-minded, and willing to adjust your own perspective if necessary.

10. **Consider professional help if needed:** If you find it challenging to communicate effectively or if conflicts persist, consider seeking the assistance of a couples' therapist or relationship counselor. A neutral third party can provide guidance and facilitate productive conversations.

Remember, healthy communication is a vital component of any successful relationship. By approaching discussions with the right attitude, active listening, and respectful communication, you can increase the chances of getting your point across while maintaining a strong connection with your partner.

Chapter 34

Physical emotional verbal violence in a relationship does not work in regards to communicating.

Trying to understand physical, emotional, and verbal violence in a relationship does not work. In fact, violence or abuse of any kind is detrimental to both individuals involved and can have long-lasting negative effects.

In healthy relationships, trust, respect, communication, and understanding are key components. Violence, whether physical, emotional, or verbal, goes against these principles and can create a toxic and harmful environment. It undermines the well-being and safety of the individuals involved and can lead to a cycle of abuse.

Physical violence involves any form of physical harm or aggression, such as hitting, slapping, pushing, or any other physical act that causes physical pain or injury. Emotional violence involves manipulating, controlling, or demeaning behaviors that undermine one's self-esteem and emotional well-being. Verbal violence includes insults, threats, yelling, and other forms of verbal aggression meant to intimidate or belittle the other person.

Not only do these forms of violence cause immediate harm, but they can also have long-term consequences for the victims, including physical injuries, emotional trauma, low self-esteem, anxiety, depression, and even post-traumatic stress disorder (PTSD). It is important for individuals to recognize the signs of an abusive relationship and seek help and support to break free from such harmful dynamics.

In any healthy relationship, open communication, mutual respect, empathy, and non-violent conflict resolution strategies should be practiced. It is essential to prioritize the well-being and safety of both individuals involved and to foster an environment of love, trust, and support. If you or someone you know is experiencing violence or abuse in a relationship, it is important to reach out to a trusted friend, family member, or professional organization for help and support.

Chapter 35

Being aware of red flags in relationships in regards to wolves and sheep clothing

When it comes to relationships, the phrase "wolves in sheep's clothing" refers to individuals who appear harmless or kind on the surface but actually have malicious intentions. These people often conceal their true nature behind a facade, making it challenging to identify their true motives. To protect yourself from potential harm or manipulation, it's essential to be aware of red flags or warning signs that might indicate someone is not who they appear to be.

Here are some common red flags to watch out for in relationships:

1. **Manipulative behavior:** Look for signs of manipulation, such as guilt-tripping, gaslighting, or constantly trying to control or influence your decisions.

2. **Inconsistent behavior:** Pay attention to inconsistencies in their words and actions. If someone frequently contradicts themselves or their behavior doesn't align with their words, it may be a warning sign.

3. **Lack of empathy:** If they consistently disregard your feelings, show little empathy, or dismiss your concerns, it may indicate a lack of emotional support and consideration.

4. **Excessive jealousy or possessiveness:** While a certain degree of jealousy is normal in relationships, extreme jealousy or possessiveness can be a sign of control issues or insecurity.

5. **Dishonesty:** If you catch them lying or notice discrepancies in their stories, it's crucial to be cautious. Trust is a fundamental aspect of any healthy relationship.

6. **Isolation from friends and family:** Be wary if they consistently try to isolate you from your loved ones or discourage you from spending time with them. This behavior can be a tactic to gain control over you.

7. **Lack of accountability:** If they refuse to take responsibility for their actions, constantly blame others, or never apologize for their mistakes, it can be a sign of an unhealthy dynamic.

8. **Intense mood swings:** Rapid and extreme mood swings can be indicative of underlying emotional instability, which can impact the relationship.

9. **Verbal or physical abuse:** Any form of abuse, be it verbal, emotional, or physical, is unacceptable and should never be tolerated.

10. **Lack of respect for boundaries:** Pay attention to whether they consistently disregard your boundaries or attempt to push them. Respect for personal boundaries is crucial in a healthy relationship.

Remember, identifying red flags is only the first step. If you notice any of these warning signs, it's important to trust your instincts, prioritize your well-being, and consider seeking support from trusted friends, family, or professionals.

Chapter 36

Traits of domestic violence:

D omestic violence refers to a pattern of abusive behavior within an intimate relationship, where one person seeks to exert power and control over the other. It can occur in various forms, including physical, sexual, emotional, and psychological abuse. While every case is unique, there are some common traits or characteristics often associated with domestic violence. It's important to note that these traits may not be present in every case, and the presence of these traits does not necessarily mean that domestic violence is occurring. However, they can serve as red flags or warning signs.

Here are some traits of domestic violence:

1. **Physical aggression:** This involves the use of physical force or violence, such as hitting, slapping, choking, or physically restraining the victim.

2. **Emotional and psychological abuse:** This includes behaviors aimed at undermining the victim's self-esteem, manipulating their emotions, and exerting control. Examples include constant criticism, humiliation, intimidation, threats, and isolation from friends and family.

3. **Sexual coercion:** This involves forcing or pressuring the victim into engaging in unwanted sexual activities or behaviors without their consent.

4. **Power and control:** Domestic violence often stems from a desire to establish power and control over the victim. The abuser may use various tactics, such as intimidation, threats, and controlling the victim's finances, to maintain dominance.

5. **Jealousy and possessiveness:** The abuser may display extreme jealousy, monitoring the victim's activities, isolating them from others, and accusing them of infidelity without evidence.

6. **Escalation of violence:** Domestic violence tends to escalate over time. What might start as minor incidents can gradually become more frequent and severe, with the abuser employing increasingly violent tactics.

7. **Blaming the victim:** The abuser often shifts blame onto the victim, making them feel responsible for the abusive behavior or its consequences. This can create feelings of guilt, shame, and confusion, making it harder for the victim to seek help.

8. **Cycle of abuse:** Domestic violence often follows a cycle, which typically includes a tension-building phase, an explosive or violent incident, and a reconciliation or remorse phase. This cycle can repeat itself unless intervention occurs.

9. **Isolation:** The abuser may isolate the victim from their support systems, including friends, family, and other sources of help. This isolation makes it harder for the victim to seek assistance or escape the abusive situation.

10. **Threats and intimidation:** Abusers may use threats of violence against the victim, their loved ones, or even themselves

as a means of control. These threats can be both explicit and implicit.

It's crucial to understand that domestic violence is a complex issue, and every situation is unique. If you or someone you know is experiencing domestic violence, it's important to seek help from professionals, such as counselors, therapists, or helplines specializing in domestic violence support.

Chapter 37

Relationships that are toxic but the man still want to be intimate but the woman doesn't

In a toxic relationship, it's important to prioritize the well-being and safety of all parties involved. If one person wants to be intimate while the other does not, it's crucial to respect boundaries and engage in open communication to address the underlying issues.

Here are some steps to consider:

1. **Self-reflection:** Both individuals need to reflect on the reasons behind their desires and boundaries. Understanding personal needs, concerns, and emotional states can help facilitate open dialogue.

2. **Communication:** Have an honest and compassionate conversation about the situation. Express your feelings, concerns, and boundaries clearly, allowing each other to share their perspectives without judgment.

3. **Seek professional help:** Consider involving a couple's therapist or counselor who specializes in toxic relationships. A professional can help navigate the complexities of the relationship, identify unhealthy patterns, and provide guidance on improving communication and establishing healthier boundaries.

4. **Establish boundaries:** It's crucial to establish and respect each other's boundaries. Boundaries can include physical intimacy, emotional space, and personal autonomy. Clearly defining and respecting these boundaries can help create a safer and healthier environment.

5. **Evaluate the relationship:** Take a step back and assess the overall health of the relationship. If the toxicity is pervasive and detrimental to the well-being of either individual, it may be necessary to consider ending the relationship for the sake of personal growth and happiness.

Remember, every situation is unique, and seeking individualized advice from a professional is recommended to address specific circumstances.

Chapter 38

This is What happens when in a toxic relationship when you let fear and her little sister anger in A toxic relationship.

When fear and anger enter into a toxic relationship, they can exacerbate the negative dynamics and contribute to further deterioration.

Here's what typically happens when these emotions are present:

1. Escalation of negative behaviors: Fear and anger can intensify unhealthy patterns within the relationship. Fear may make you more submissive or compliant, allowing the toxic behavior to persist. Anger, on the other hand, can lead to increased confrontations, aggression, and even violence. Both emotions can create a vicious cycle of toxic interactions.

2. Communication breakdown: Fear and anger often hinder effective communication. Fear may prevent you from expressing your true feelings, needs, and boundaries, making it difficult to address the toxic behavior in a healthy manner. Anger, if not managed properly, can lead to aggressive or defensive communication, which further hampers understanding and resolution.

3. Emotional and psychological harm: In a toxic relationship, fear and anger can take a toll on your emotional well-being.

Constant fear can lead to anxiety, low self-esteem, and even depression. Anger, when not expressed or managed appropriately, can result in feelings of resentment, bitterness, and emotional exhaustion. Both emotions can contribute to a deteriorating sense of self-worth and overall mental health.

4. Reinforcement of unhealthy dynamics: When fear and anger become prominent in a toxic relationship, they reinforce the power imbalances and toxic patterns already present. Fear may keep you trapped in the relationship, making it difficult to leave or set boundaries. Anger, if not addressed constructively, can perpetuate a cycle of retaliation, blame, and further toxic behavior.

5. Deterioration of physical health: Prolonged exposure to fear and anger can have detrimental effects on your physical health. Chronic stress resulting from fear and ongoing conflict can lead to increased blood pressure, weakened immune system, headaches, digestive issues, and other stress-related ailments.

If you find yourself in a toxic relationship where fear and anger dominate, it is crucial to seek support and consider professional help. A therapist or counselor can assist you in navigating these emotions, developing coping strategies, and exploring options for healing or exiting the toxic relationship. Remember, your well-being and safety should always be a priority.

Chapter 39

When you're in a narcissistic relationship where your partner always says all about me and Disregard what about you and what you might be going through.

Being in a relationship with a narcissistic partner can be challenging and emotionally draining. Narcissistic individuals often have an excessive sense of self-importance, a constant need for admiration, and a lack of empathy for others. In such relationships, they tend to focus solely on their own needs and desires, disregarding those of their partner.

If you find yourself in a narcissistic relationship where your partner consistently dismisses your feelings and needs, it's essential to recognize that this behavior is not healthy or acceptable.

Here are a few suggestions on how to navigate this situation:

1. **Recognize the signs:** Educate yourself about narcissistic traits and behaviors. Understanding what you're dealing with can help you gain clarity and develop strategies to protect yourself.

2. **Set boundaries:** Establish clear boundaries and communicate your needs and expectations. Be assertive but calm when discussing your concerns. Narcissists may not respond

well to criticism, so try to frame your statements in a non-confrontational manner.

3. **Prioritize self-care:** Take care of yourself and prioritize your emotional well-being. Engage in activities that bring you joy and spend time with supportive friends and family. Seeking therapy or counseling can also be beneficial in navigating the challenges of a narcissistic relationship.

4. **Seek support:** Reach out to trusted friends, family, or support groups. Sharing your experiences with others who have been through similar situations can provide validation and guidance.

5. **Consider leaving the relationship:** In severe cases, it may be necessary to consider ending the relationship. Remember that you deserve to be in a healthy and fulfilling partnership. Leaving a narcissistic relationship can be difficult, so having a support network and professional guidance can be invaluable.

Remember, you cannot change a narcissistic person, as their behavior is deeply ingrained. Your focus should be on your own well-being and taking steps to protect yourself from emotional harm.

Chapter 40

Recognizing red flags in a toxic relationship.

Recognizing red flags in a toxic relationship is essential for your emotional well-being and personal growth.

Here are some common red flags to watch out for:

1. **Lack of respect:** A toxic partner may consistently disrespect your boundaries, opinions, or feelings. They may mock you, belittle you, or dismiss your thoughts and emotions.

2. **Controlling behavior:** If your partner tries to control your actions, decisions, or who you spend time with, it's a sign of a toxic relationship. They may isolate you from friends and family, monitor your activities, or make you feel guilty for asserting your independence.

3. **Manipulation and gaslighting:** Toxic individuals often manipulate situations to make you doubt your own perceptions, memories, or sanity. They may twist the truth, deny their actions, or blame you for their behavior. Gaslighting can leave you feeling confused, anxious, and unsure of yourself.

4. **Lack of support:** In a healthy relationship, both partners support each other's goals and dreams. However, toxic partners may be unsupportive, dismissive, or even sabotage your efforts to grow and succeed.

5. **Constant criticism:** Toxic individuals frequently criticize and demean their partners. They may criticize your appearance, intelligence, abilities, or any aspect of your life. This constant criticism can erode your self-esteem over time.

6. **Emotional or physical abuse:** Any form of abuse, whether emotional, physical, or sexual, is a severe red flag. This includes verbal insults, threats, physical violence, or coercive behavior. If you experience abuse, it's crucial to seek help immediately.

7. **Lack of accountability:** Toxic partners often refuse to take responsibility for their actions. They may deflect blame onto you, make excuses, or deny any wrongdoing. They may also refuse to apologize sincerely or show genuine remorse.

8. **Unhealthy jealousy and possessiveness:** While some jealousy is normal in relationships, excessive jealousy and possessiveness are red flags. If your partner tries to control who you talk to, where you go, or accuses you of infidelity without reason, it indicates a toxic dynamic.

9. **Emotional roller coaster:** Toxic relationships are often characterized by extreme highs and lows. Your partner may shower you with affection one moment and then become cold, distant, or angry the next. This instability can be emotionally draining and create a constant state of anxiety.

10. **Isolation from loved ones:** Toxic partners may try to isolate you from your friends and family. They may discourage or prevent you from spending time with loved ones, making you dependent on them for emotional support and validation.

Remember, one or two red flags don't necessarily mean you're in a toxic relationship, but if you notice several of these signs consistently, it's crucial to evaluate the health of your relationship and consider seeking support from trusted friends, family, or a professional counselor.

Chapter 41

When talking about domestic violence it doesn't only include men and women that also includes children how to understand the characteristics of childhood domestic violence.

Childhood domestic violence refers to situations where children witness or are exposed to domestic violence between their parents or caregivers. It can have severe and long-lasting effects on a child's physical, emotional, and psychological well-being. Understanding the characteristics of childhood domestic violence can help identify and address the issue effectively.

Here are some key indicators:

1. **Physical signs:** Children exposed to domestic violence may exhibit physical signs such as unexplained bruises, injuries, or frequent accidents. These injuries may occur as a result of being caught in the crossfire or deliberately targeted during violent episodes.

2. **Emotional and behavioral changes:** Children who witness domestic violence may display significant emotional and behavioral changes. They may become anxious, fearful, or withdrawn. They might exhibit excessive aggression, anger, or act out in school or other social settings. They may also have difficulty concentrating, experience nightmares, or develop regressive behaviors.

3. **Social withdrawal and isolation:** Children exposed to domestic violence may isolate themselves from peers, friends, and social activities. They might struggle with forming and maintaining healthy relationships due to a lack of trust or fear of conflict.

4. **Poor academic performance:** The stress and trauma of witnessing domestic violence can interfere with a child's ability to focus on their studies, leading to academic difficulties. They may struggle with concentration, have frequent absences, or experience a decline in their overall performance.

5. **Emotional regulation difficulties:** Children exposed to domestic violence may have difficulty regulating their emotions. They may exhibit intense mood swings, have difficulty expressing their emotions appropriately, or have trouble identifying and managing their feelings.

6. **Hypervigilance:** Children in households with domestic violence often develop a sense of hypervigilance, where they are constantly on edge and alert to potential danger. They may be excessively watchful, easily startled, or have difficulty relaxing and feeling safe.

7. **Internalized blame and guilt:** Children who witness domestic violence often internalize feelings of blame and guilt. They may believe that they caused the violence or that it is their responsibility to fix the situation. This self-blame can have long-lasting emotional effects.

8. **Developmental delays:** Children exposed to domestic violence may experience delays in their developmental milestones.

This can manifest as delays in speech, motor skills, cognitive abilities, or emotional maturity.

If you suspect or observe signs of childhood domestic violence, it is crucial to take the situation seriously and seek help. Contact local child protective services, a trusted teacher or school counselor, a healthcare professional, or a child advocacy organization to report the situation and seek guidance on how to provide support and protection for the child.

Chapter 42

I remember when I was a child going to the domestic violence from my mother and father there was times where if I felt went to sleep everything will be OK when I woke but nothing changed how does the child deal with that.

Experienced domestic violence as a child. Dealing with the aftermath of such traumatic experiences can be challenging.

Here are some strategies that can help children cope with the effects of domestic violence:

1. **Seek support:** It's important for children to have a support system they can rely on. Reach out to a trusted adult, such as a teacher, counselor, family member, or friend, who can provide a listening ear, emotional support, and guidance. Professional therapists who specialize in trauma can also be immensely helpful in navigating the healing process.

2. **Express feelings:** Encourage the child to express their emotions in a safe and supportive environment. This can be through talking, writing in a journal, drawing, or engaging in other creative outlets. Validating their feelings and letting them know it's okay to experience a range of emotions can be empowering.

3. **Psychoeducation:** Help the child understand that the violence they witnessed was not their fault. Provide age-appropriate

information about domestic violence and explain that it is the responsibility of adults to create a safe and healthy environment.

4. **Safety planning:** Work with trusted adults to create safety plans that the child can follow in case of emergencies or if they feel unsafe. Having a plan can help reduce anxiety and empower the child with a sense of control.

5. **Develop coping skills:** Teach and encourage the child to develop healthy coping mechanisms to manage stress and difficult emotions. This can include deep breathing exercises, mindfulness techniques, engaging in hobbies and activities they enjoy, or seeking solace in nature.

6. **Establish routines and stability:** Creating a stable and predictable environment can help children regain a sense of safety and security. Establish consistent routines for daily activities, such as mealtimes, bedtime, and homework. Providing stability and structure can be immensely reassuring.

7. **Encourage self-care:** Teach the child the importance of self-care and self-compassion. Encourage activities that promote their physical, emotional, and mental well-being, such as exercise, spending time with supportive friends, engaging in hobbies, and practicing relaxation techniques.

8. **Encourage healthy relationships:** Help the child build healthy relationships with peers and positive role models. Encourage them to engage in activities that promote socialization, teamwork, and a sense of belonging.

9. **Professional help:** Consider involving a mental health professional experienced in trauma and child development. Therapy can provide a safe space for the child to process their experiences, develop coping strategies, and work through any lingering effects of the trauma.

Remember, healing from childhood trauma takes time, and each individual's journey is unique. Patience, understanding, and ongoing support are essential in helping children navigate the challenges they may face.

Chapter 43

A lot of adults don't understand that children know about the domestic violence going on in their home but they don't talk about it how can you talk to a channel to help them to understand the reality of the situation with regards to domestic violence in the home.

If you want to raise awareness and help adults understand the reality of domestic violence in the home.

Here are some suggestions for effectively communicating your message:

1. **Choose the right channel:** Consider using a medium that reaches a wide audience, such as social media platforms, blogs, or local newspapers. You could also consider approaching organizations or community groups that focus on domestic violence issues.

2. **Use personal stories:** Share real stories or experiences of children who have witnessed domestic violence. Personal narratives can be powerful tools for conveying the emotional impact and realities of the situation.

3. **Provide facts and statistics:** Presenting factual information about the prevalence and consequences of domestic violence can help dispel misconceptions and highlight the seriousness

of the issue. Include data from reputable sources or studies to support your claims.

4. **Address common misconceptions:** Many adults may hold misconceptions about domestic violence, such as believing that children are unaware of the situation. Use your platform to correct these misconceptions and provide accurate information about the impact on children.

5. **Offer resources and support:** Include information about local helplines, shelters, counseling services, or other resources that can assist both adults and children affected by domestic violence. Encourage those who need help to seek support.

6. **Promote empathy and understanding:** Encourage your audience to empathize with the experiences of children witnessing domestic violence. Help them understand the emotional toll it can take on children and the long-term consequences they may face.

7. **Collaborate with professionals:** Reach out to professionals working in the field of domestic violence, such as therapists, social workers, or advocates, and ask them to contribute their expertise or share practical advice for supporting children in these situations.

8. **Engage with your audience:** Encourage dialogue and open discussions around domestic violence. Respond to comments and questions, and create a safe space for people to share their experiences or seek guidance.

Remember, raising awareness about domestic violence requires ongoing effort and collaboration. It may take time to change people's perceptions, but by continuing to educate and advocate, you can make a difference in helping adults understand the reality of domestic violence in the home.

Chapter 44

Dealing with domestic violence in a blended family relationship.

Dealing with domestic violence in a blended family relationship is a serious and delicate matter that requires careful consideration and action.

Here are some steps to help address this issue:

1. **Ensure safety:** The safety of all family members, especially those who may be victims of domestic violence, should be the top priority. If anyone is in immediate danger, contact local law enforcement or emergency services.

2. **Seek professional help:** Reach out to a professional counselor, therapist, or social worker who specializes in domestic violence. They can provide guidance, support, and resources to help address the situation.

3. **Encourage open communication:** Create a safe and non-judgmental environment where family members can openly discuss their concerns and experiences. Encourage them to express their feelings and thoughts without fear of reprisal.

4. **Educate yourself:** Gain knowledge about domestic violence, its causes, effects, and available resources. Understanding the dynamics of domestic violence can empower you to provide better support to those affected.

5. **Support the victims:** Victims of domestic violence may need emotional support, reassurance, and validation. Listen to their experiences without judgment, respect their choices, and encourage them to seek help when they are ready.

6. **Develop a safety plan:** Work with the victims and professionals to develop a safety plan that outlines steps to ensure their well-being. This may involve identifying safe places to go, emergency contacts, and strategies for managing potentially dangerous situations.

7. **Involve legal authorities if necessary:** If the situation escalates or if there is a risk of harm, it may be necessary to involve law enforcement or seek legal protection through restraining orders or other legal measures.

8. **Promote counseling and therapy:** Encourage family members, both victims, and perpetrators, to participate in counseling or therapy to address the underlying issues contributing to the domestic violence. This can help break the cycle of abuse and facilitate healing.

9. **Foster a supportive network:** Reach out to support groups or organizations that specialize in domestic violence. These groups can provide additional guidance, resources, and a network of people who have faced similar situations.

10. **Create a safe and nurturing environment:** Foster an environment of respect, empathy, and open communication within the blended family. Promote healthy relationships, positive role modeling, and conflict resolution skills.

Remember, dealing with domestic violence is a complex issue, and it's important to involve professionals who can provide the necessary expertise and support.

Chapter 45

How to understand the warning signs of a domestic violence or toxic relationship.

Understanding the warning signs of a domestic violence or toxic relationship is crucial for your well-being and safety.

Here are some common signs to be aware of:

1. **Excessive jealousy and possessiveness:** Your partner may constantly monitor your activities, isolate you from friends and family, or accuse you of infidelity without any evidence.

2. **Controlling behavior:** They may exert control over various aspects of your life, such as your finances, daily schedule, or decision-making. They might make all the important choices without considering your input.

3. **Verbal or emotional abuse:** This can include insults, humiliation, constant criticism, and belittling remarks that undermine your self-esteem. They may manipulate your emotions to gain power and control over you.

4. **Physical violence or threats:** This is a major red flag. Any form of physical harm, including pushing, slapping, punching, or threats of violence, is unacceptable and dangerous.

5. **Intimidation and coercion:** They may use threats, intimidation, or coercion to make you comply with their demands or control your behavior.

6. **Unpredictability and mood swings:** If your partner's behavior fluctuates between extreme kindness and extreme anger or aggression, it can be a sign of a toxic relationship.

7. **Isolation and monitoring:** They might isolate you from friends, family, and support networks. They could monitor your phone calls, texts, or online activity without your consent.

8. **Blaming and shifting responsibility:** They often refuse to take responsibility for their actions and instead blame you or external factors for their behavior.

9. **Financial abuse:** They may control all the finances, restrict your access to money, or prevent you from working or pursuing financial independence.

10. **Gaslighting:** This manipulative tactic involves distorting your perception of reality, making you question your own sanity, memory, or judgment.

11. **Threats of self-harm or suicide:** Some abusers may use threats of self-harm or suicide to manipulate and control their partner emotionally.

It's important to remember that these signs can vary in intensity and frequency. If you notice any of these warning signs in your relationship, it's crucial to seek help and support. Reach out to a trusted friend, family member, helpline, or a professional counselor who can provide guidance and assistance in navigating the situation safely.

Chapter 46

My perspective of the reason why love shouldn't hate is when you're with someone and they said that you they love you it shouldn't hurt.

I understand your perspective that when someone says they love you, it shouldn't hurt. Love is generally associated with positive emotions, care, and support. However, it's important to recognize that relationships and emotions are complex, and sometimes even in loving relationships, hurtful situations can occur.

Misunderstandings, disagreements, and conflicts can arise between people, even when they love each other. Sometimes, hurtful things are said or done unintentionally due to a lack of communication, differing perspectives, or personal struggles. It's crucial to address these issues openly and honestly, with the intention of resolving conflicts and strengthening the relationship.

However, it's also important to note that love should never be accompanied by abusive or manipulative behavior. If someone consistently hurts you physically, emotionally, or psychologically, it's not a healthy or loving relationship. In such cases, it's essential to prioritize your well-being and seek support from trusted friends, family, or professionals.

Ultimately, love should be a source of happiness, respect, and growth. It involves understanding, compassion, and forgiveness. While it's unrealistic to expect a relationship to be completely free of any hurt or pain, it's important to strive for healthy and loving dynamics where conflicts can be resolved through open communication, empathy, and mutual respect.

Chapter 47

E motional difficulties enter a relationship such as insecurity, narcissistic paranoid schizophrenic behavior comes into a relationship that wasn't brought up in the beginning of the relationship can cause difficulties in a relationship what should one do in order to handle such mental behaviors.

Handling emotional difficulties and mental health issues within a relationship can be challenging.

These are several steps you can take to navigate these challenges:

1. **Educate Yourself:** Learn about the specific mental health issues involved, such as insecurity, narcissism, and paranoid schizophrenia. Understanding these conditions can help you gain insight into the behaviors and challenges you may encounter.

2. **Encourage Professional Help:** Suggest that your partner seek professional support from mental health experts such as therapists, counselors, or psychiatrists. These professionals can provide appropriate diagnosis, treatment, and support tailored to their specific needs.

3. **Foster Open Communication:** Encourage open and honest communication with your partner about their mental health struggles. Create a safe and non-judgmental space for them

to share their feelings, concerns, and experiences. Active listening and empathy are essential during these discussions.

4. **Set Boundaries:** Establish clear boundaries and communicate your needs and limits within the relationship. Ensure that your own mental health and well-being are prioritized as well. Boundaries can help protect your emotional and physical safety while maintaining a healthy relationship dynamic.

5. **Seek Support for Yourself:** Dealing with a partner's mental health challenges can be emotionally draining. Find support for yourself through friends, family, or support groups. Consider seeking therapy for yourself to help manage your own emotions and navigate the complexities of the relationship.

6. **Encourage Self-Care:** Encourage your partner to engage in self-care activities that promote their mental well-being, such as exercise, hobbies, or mindfulness practices. Engaging in healthy habits can contribute positively to their overall mental health.

7. **Practice Patience and Understanding:** Remember that managing mental health issues takes time and effort. Be patient with your partner and understand that their behaviors may be influenced by their condition. Offer support and reassurance, but also maintain healthy boundaries.

8. **Evaluate the Relationship:** Assess whether the relationship is healthy and sustainable in the long term. Consider the impact of your partner's mental health issues on both of you and evaluate if you can maintain a healthy, fulfilling relationship. Sometimes, despite efforts, it may be necessary

to prioritize your own well-being and make difficult decisions regarding the future of the relationship.

Remember, it is crucial to prioritize your own mental health and well-being in any relationship. If you feel unsafe, unsupported, or overwhelmed, do not hesitate to seek professional advice or guidance from a therapist or counselor.

Chapter 48

When dealing in a controlling and toxic relationship what is the best time to contact authorities before it's too late.

In a controlling and toxic relationship, it can be challenging to determine the best time to contact authorities, as every situation is unique and depends on various factors. However, if you feel that your safety or the safety of others is at immediate risk, you should contact the authorities as soon as possible.

Here are some indicators that may suggest contacting authorities:

1. **Physical violence or threats:** If you are experiencing physical abuse or threats of harm, it is crucial to contact the authorities immediately. Your safety should be the top priority.

2. **Emotional or psychological abuse:** If you are enduring consistent emotional manipulation, verbal abuse, or psychological torment, it can significantly impact your well-being. If you feel trapped or unable to escape the situation, consider contacting the authorities for guidance and support.

3. **Stalking or harassment:** If your partner is engaging in stalking behaviors or persistent harassment, such as following you, tracking your movements, or sending threatening messages, it is important to involve the authorities to ensure your safety.

4. **Financial exploitation:** If your partner is exploiting you financially, preventing you from accessing your own money, or coercing you into financial decisions against your will, seeking legal assistance or contacting the authorities can help protect your rights.

5. **Child abuse or endangerment:** If children are involved and you suspect they are being abused or endangered in any way, it is crucial to report the situation to the authorities immediately. Child protective services can intervene to ensure the well-being and safety of the children.

Remember, it is always advisable to seek professional advice from domestic violence hotlines, counseling services, or legal professionals who specialize in dealing with such situations. They can provide you with guidance tailored to your specific circumstances and help you understand the available options and resources.

Chapter 49

Why are so many women afraid to talk to their family in regards to domestic violence in their life?

There are several reasons why many women may be afraid to talk to their family about domestic violence in their lives. It's important to note that every situation is unique, and individuals may have different reasons for their fear.

However, here are some common factors that contribute to this fear:

1. **Fear of retribution:** Women who are experiencing domestic violence often fear retaliation from their abusers if they disclose their situation. Abusers may use threats, coercion, or physical violence to maintain control, making it difficult for victims to speak out.

2. **Shame and stigma:** Society's perception of domestic violence can create a sense of shame and stigma for victims. They may worry about being judged, blamed, or disbelieved by family members if they disclose the abuse. This fear of judgment can be especially strong in cultures or communities that stigmatize victims or prioritize family reputation over individual well-being.

3. **Dependency on the abuser:** Many women in abusive relationships may be financially or emotionally dependent on

their abusers. They may fear losing financial support, custody of their children, or the stability of their family unit if they speak out about the abuse. The abuser may also manipulate the victim into believing that they are solely responsible for the abuse or that they will not be believed or supported by others.

4. **Lack of support or understanding:** Some women may have had previous negative experiences when disclosing abuse, such as not being believed or receiving inadequate support. These experiences can make them hesitant to reach out to their families for help. They may fear being dismissed, invalidated, or blamed for the abuse, leading to a sense of isolation and mistrust.

5. **Cultural and religious factors:** Cultural or religious beliefs and norms can play a significant role in inhibiting women from talking about domestic violence. Some cultures or religious communities may prioritize maintaining harmony within the family or discourage discussing private matters outside the household, which can discourage victims from seeking support.

It's important to create safe spaces and support systems where women feel comfortable discussing domestic violence. Encouraging open dialogue, providing access to resources, and promoting awareness can help break the silence surrounding this issue and empower women to seek help and support.

Chapter 50

When in our relationship and your partner says that they love you but they don't trust you.

When your partner says they love you but don't trust you, it can be a complex and challenging situation. Trust is an essential component of a healthy and strong relationship, and when it is lacking, it can create significant issues and strain the bond between partners. It's important to address this issue and communicate openly to understand the reasons behind their lack of trust and work towards resolving it.

Here are some steps you can consider:

1. **Open and honest communication:** Have a calm and non-confrontational conversation with your partner about their concerns and why they feel a lack of trust. Encourage them to express their feelings and listen attentively without becoming defensive.

2. **Understand their perspective**: Try to empathize with your partner's feelings and perspective. Trust issues can stem from past experiences, insecurities, or other reasons. Understanding their concerns can help you find ways to rebuild trust.

3. **Self-reflection**: Reflect on your actions and behavior to determine if there are any valid reasons for your partner's lack

of trust. Be open to self-improvement and take responsibility for any mistakes you may have made.

4. **Rebuilding trust**: Rebuilding trust takes time and effort from both partners. Be consistent in your words and actions, and follow through on any commitments you make. Be transparent and honest in your communication and behavior.

5. **Seek professional help if needed**: If the lack of trust persists despite your best efforts, consider seeking couples therapy or counseling. A trained professional can help facilitate communication, explore underlying issues, and provide guidance on rebuilding trust.

Remember, trust is not built overnight, and it requires ongoing effort and commitment from both partners. It's important to be patient, understanding, and willing to work together to address the trust issues and strengthen your relationship.

Chapter 51

How to deal with the relationship where the woman was sexually assaulted and trying to get over it and still maintain a relationship with her partner.

Dealing with the aftermath of sexual assault requires sensitivity, understanding, and patience. If you're in a relationship with someone who has experienced sexual assault and you want to support them.

Here are some suggestions:

1. **Encourage open communication:** Create a safe and non-judgmental environment where your partner feels comfortable sharing their thoughts, fears, and emotions. Let them know that you are there to listen and support them.

2. **Educate yourself:** Learn about the effects of sexual assault, such as post-traumatic stress disorder (**PTSD**), anxiety, depression, and trust issues. Understanding the impact of trauma can help you be more empathetic and responsive.

3. **Believe and validate their experiences:** Trust and believe your partner when they share their assault experience. Never question or doubt their account of what happened. Validate their feelings, emotions, and reactions, even if you don't fully understand them.

4. **Respect their boundaries:** It's essential to respect your partner's boundaries and allow them to set the pace for physical and emotional intimacy. Avoid pressuring them into any activities that make them uncomfortable.

5. **Encourage professional help:** Suggest that your partner seeks professional help from a therapist or counselor who specializes in trauma and sexual assault. Therapy can provide them with a safe space to process their emotions and develop coping strategies.

6. **Be patient and understanding:** Recovery from sexual assault takes time, and healing is not linear. There may be moments when your partner experiences triggers or setbacks. Be patient, understanding, and supportive throughout their healing journey.

7. **Encourage self-care:** Help your partner prioritize self-care activities that promote their well-being. This could include engaging in hobbies, practicing mindfulness or meditation, exercising, or spending time with loved ones.

8. **Avoid victim-blaming or judgment:** It's important to avoid blaming your partner or making them feel guilty for the assault. Focus on supporting their healing rather than questioning their actions or decisions leading up to the incident.

9. **Be a source of stability and safety:** Consistency and reliability can help your partner rebuild trust and feel safe. Be dependable, keep your promises, and be there for them when they need you.

10. **Seek support for yourself:** Supporting a survivor of sexual assault can be emotionally challenging. It's vital that you also take care of your own well-being by seeking support from friends, family, or a therapist.

Remember, every survivor's journey is unique, and what works for one person may not work for another. Regularly checking in with your partner and openly discussing their needs and boundaries can help you navigate the challenges together.

Chapter 52

B eing in a relationship as a blended family.

Being in a relationship as a blended family can present
unique challenges and rewards. A blended family typically consists
of a couple and their children from previous relationships, coming
together to form a new family unit.

**Here are some considerations and tips for navigating a
successful relationship as a blended family:**

1. **Open and honest communication:** Communication is key
   in any relationship, but it becomes even more important in a
   blended family. Encourage open and honest communication
   between all family members, including the children. Create a
   safe space where everyone feels comfortable expressing their
   thoughts and emotions.

2. **Patience and understanding:** It takes time for family
   members to adjust to the new dynamics and build relationships
   with one another. Be patient and understanding as everyone
   adapts to the changes. Recognize that each person may have
   different needs and emotions during the transition.

3. **Respect boundaries:** It's essential to respect everyone's
   boundaries, including the children's. Understand that each
   person may have different levels of comfort and may need

space or time to adjust. Respect their need for privacy and personal space.

4. **Establish clear roles and expectations:** Discuss and establish clear roles and expectations for each family member. This can help reduce conflicts and confusion. For example, determine how parenting responsibilities will be shared and how discipline will be handled.

5. **Create new family traditions:** Blend the family's existing traditions with new ones. This can help create a sense of unity and belonging. Involve all family members in the process of creating and celebrating these traditions.

6. **Seek professional help if needed:** If you're facing significant challenges or conflicts within your blended family, consider seeking the guidance of a family therapist or counselor. They can provide valuable insights and strategies to help navigate specific issues.

7. **Foster individual relationships:** Encourage and support the development of individual relationships between the stepparent and stepchildren. Allow these relationships to grow naturally, without forcing them. Building trust and rapport takes time.

8. **Be flexible and adaptable:** Blended families often require flexibility and adaptability. Recognize that circumstances may change, and adjustments may be necessary along the way. Embrace the opportunity to learn and grow as a family.

Remember, building a successful blended family takes time, effort, and a willingness to work together. By fostering open communication, mutual respect, and a supportive environment, you can create a loving and harmonious relationship as a blended family.

Chapter 53

Entering a relationship with someone that has mental health issues.

Entering a relationship with someone who has mental health issues can present unique challenges. However, with understanding, compassion, and open communication, it is possible to build a supportive and fulfilling relationship.

Here are some considerations to keep in mind:

1. **Education and Awareness:** Educate yourself about your partner's mental health condition. Learn about the symptoms, triggers, and treatment options. This knowledge will help you better understand their experiences and provide appropriate support.

2. **Empathy and Compassion:** Be empathetic and compassionate towards your partner. Understand that their mental health issues may affect their thoughts, emotions, and behavior. Show understanding and patience during difficult times and avoid stigmatizing their condition.

3. **Open Communication:** Encourage open and honest communication. Create a safe space where your partner feels comfortable discussing their mental health concerns. Be a good listener and validate their feelings without judgment.

4. **Support and Encouragement:** Offer support and encouragement in their journey towards recovery. Be there for them when they need someone to talk to or when they require practical assistance. Encourage them to seek professional help and accompany them to therapy sessions if they desire.

5. **Boundaries and Self-Care:** Take care of your own well-being as well. Establish healthy boundaries and communicate your needs within the relationship. Understand that you cannot solely be responsible for your partner's mental health. Encourage them to develop their coping strategies and engage in self-care practices.

6. **Seek Professional Help:** Encourage your partner to seek professional help from therapists, psychiatrists, or support groups. Mental health professionals can provide appropriate guidance, treatment, and coping strategies for your partner's specific condition.

7. **Patience and Flexibility:** Understand that recovery from mental health issues can be a complex and ongoing process. It may require patience, flexibility, and a willingness to adapt to the challenges that may arise. Celebrate the small victories and provide reassurance during setbacks.

Remember, each person's experience with mental health issues is unique, so it is important to be responsive to your partner's individual needs. By fostering a supportive and understanding environment, you can create a strong foundation for a healthy relationship.

Chapter 54

E ntering a new relationship and you have a guy best friend but your new partner does not agree with your relationship with him.

Navigating relationships can be complex, especially when it comes to balancing friendships with new romantic partners. It's important to approach the situation with open communication and understanding.

Here are a few suggestions on how to handle this scenario:

1. **Communicate openly:** Have an honest conversation with your new partner about your friendship with your guy best friend. Share the history of your friendship, its importance to you, and the boundaries that exist within that friendship. Encourage your partner to express their concerns and listen to their perspective without becoming defensive.

2. **Understand your partner's concerns:** Try to empathize with your partner's point of view and understand their concerns. They might be feeling insecure, threatened, or worried about the level of emotional intimacy between you and your best friend. Addressing their concerns can help alleviate their worries and build trust in your new relationship.

3. **Establish boundaries:** Discuss and establish clear boundaries with both your best friend and your partner. This

may include reducing the frequency of interactions, being transparent about plans and activities, or involving your partner in group outings with your friend to help build trust and familiarity.

4. **Include your partner in activities:** Encourage your partner to spend time with you and your best friend together. This can help them see the dynamic of your friendship and reduce any insecurities they may have. As your partner gets to know your friend, they may develop a better understanding and become more comfortable with your relationship.

5. **Reassure your partner:** Reassure your partner of your commitment to the new relationship. Show them through your actions that they are a priority in your life and that your friendship with your best friend does not threaten your romantic connection. Regularly communicate your feelings for your partner and reinforce the unique aspects of your romantic relationship.

6. **Seek compromise:** If your partner continues to express concerns, try to find a compromise that respects both their feelings and the importance of your friendship. This might involve adjusting the nature or frequency of interactions with your best friend to alleviate your partner's concerns while still maintaining the friendship.

Remember, every relationship is unique, and finding a balance between friendships and romantic partnerships requires open communication, understanding, and compromise from both sides. It's essential to create an environment of trust and respect where both you and your partner feel comfortable expressing your needs and concerns.

Chapter 55

Men that are in relationships that are not satisfied with just one woman.

Men, like women, have diverse needs and desires when it comes to relationships. Some men may indeed find themselves unsatisfied with being in a monogamous relationship with just one woman. This can stem from a variety of reasons, including differences in sexual preferences, emotional needs, or a desire for variety and novelty in their romantic or sexual experiences.

It's important to recognize that not all men feel this way, and there are many men who are perfectly content and fulfilled in monogamous relationships. However, for those who do experience dissatisfaction, there are different relationship models that may better suit their needs.

1. **Open Relationships**: Some individuals enter into consensually non-monogamous relationships, where both partners agree to have additional sexual or romantic partners outside of the relationship. This allows for emotional connection and physical intimacy with multiple people while maintaining a primary relationship.

2. **Polyamory**: Polyamory is a relationship style where individuals have multiple emotional and/or sexual relationships simultaneously, with the knowledge and consent of all involved parties. In polyamorous relationships, the focus is on building

meaningful connections and fostering love and intimacy with multiple partners.

It's crucial for individuals in such situations to engage in open and honest communication with their partners. This allows for an understanding of each other's needs, boundaries, and expectations. Every relationship is unique, and what works for one couple may not work for another. Ultimately, it's essential for individuals to find relationship dynamics that align with their values, desires, and overall happiness, while ensuring that all parties involved are consenting and well-informed.

Chapter 56

When two friends has been in a relationship for a very long time even though they weren't together but they had feelings for each other and they see their friend in a toxic relationship

When two friends have had feelings for each other for a long time, even though they were not in a romantic relationship, and they observe one of them in a toxic relationship, it can be a complex and challenging situation.

Here are a few things to consider:

1. **Evaluate the situation objectively:** Assess the dynamics of the toxic relationship and determine if it genuinely poses a risk to your friend's well-being. Look for signs of emotional, physical, or psychological abuse. It's important to be sure that your concerns are valid before intervening.

2. **Communicate your concerns:** Find a suitable time and place to have an open and honest conversation with your friend. Express your worries about their well-being and provide specific examples of behaviors that you find concerning. Be supportive and non-judgmental, allowing them to share their perspective as well.

3. **Offer support:** Let your friend know that you are there for them, regardless of their choices. Sometimes people in toxic relationships may feel isolated or trapped, so offering your

support can make a significant difference. Encourage them to seek professional help, such as therapy or counseling, if necessary.

4. **Respect their choices:** Ultimately, it's your friend's decision whether to stay or leave the toxic relationship. Respect their autonomy and understand that they may have their reasons for staying. It's important not to pressure or force them to take any action they are not ready for.

5. **Encourage self-reflection:** Help your friend reflect on their own feelings and desires. Sometimes individuals in long-standing friendships with underlying romantic feelings may need time to evaluate their emotions and make decisions about their relationship. Encourage them to think about what they truly want and what would make them happy in the long run.

6. **Maintain boundaries:** As a friend, it's important to set boundaries for yourself. Supporting someone through a difficult situation can be emotionally draining, so make sure to prioritize your own well-being. Seek support from other friends or professionals if you feel overwhelmed.

Remember that every situation is unique, and there is no one-size-fits-all approach. It's important to handle the situation with empathy, respect, and understanding. If you believe your friend's safety is at immediate risk, it may be necessary to involve authorities or other appropriate.

Chapter 57

Fear and anger in a relationship is very toxic you see anger is fears Little Sister and whatever fear goes anger goes as well in this chapter I will explain to you why it's so toxic.

Fear and anger are both common emotions that can arise in relationships. While they can be challenging to navigate, it's important to address them in a healthy and constructive manner.

Here's a breakdown of fear and anger in relationships:

1. **Fear:** Fear can manifest in different ways within a relationship. Some common fears include the fear of rejection, abandonment, betrayal, or losing control. These fears may stem from past experiences, insecurities, or a lack of trust. Fear can lead to defensive behavior, emotional withdrawal, or an unwillingness to be vulnerable.

To address fear in a relationship:

- Communication: Create a safe and open environment for honest conversations about fears and insecurities. Express your concerns and listen to your partner's perspective without judgment.

- Build trust: Trust is essential for overcoming fear. Work on building trust through consistent actions, transparency, and keeping your promises.

- Seek support: If fear in the relationship becomes overwhelming or deeply rooted, consider seeking professional help such as couples therapy or individual counseling.

- Anger: Anger is a natural emotion that can arise in relationships due to various reasons, such as unmet expectations, perceived injustices, or unresolved conflicts. However, unresolved anger can be detrimental to a relationship if not managed properly.

To address anger in a relationship:

- Calm down: When anger arises, take a step back and allow yourself to calm down before engaging in a conversation. This helps prevent impulsive and hurtful reactions.

- Take responsibility: Acknowledge your own anger and take responsibility for your feelings and actions. Avoid blaming your partner solely for the situation.

- Active listening: Practice active listening to understand your partner's perspective and the underlying issues causing the anger. Validate their feelings and express empathy.

- Healthy communication: Express your anger assertively, using "I" statements to avoid attacking or demeaning your partner. Focus on finding solutions rather than escalating conflict.

- Conflict resolution: Work together to find compromises and resolve conflicts. Consider seeking professional help if the anger persists or leads to destructive patterns.

Remember, fear and anger are normal emotions, but it's crucial to address them constructively in a relationship. Open communication, empathy, and a willingness to work together can help create a healthier and more fulfilling partnership.

Chapter 58

How to recognize a wolf in sheep clothing when you begin a new relationship.

Recognizing a person who may be hiding their true intentions or character traits can be challenging, but there are several signs to watch out for when starting a new relationship.

Here are some tips to help you recognize a potential wolf in sheep's clothing:

1. **Take your time:** Rushing into a relationship can blind you to red flags. Take your time getting to know the person before committing emotionally or making any major decisions.

2. **Observe their behavior:** Pay attention to how they treat others, including friends, family, and strangers. A person's behavior towards others can be an indicator of their true character.

3. **Trust your instincts:** If something feels off or you have a gut feeling about the person, don't ignore it. Our instincts often pick up on subtle cues that our conscious mind may miss.

4. **Look for inconsistencies:** Notice if their words and actions align. If someone says one thing but consistently acts differently, it could be a sign that they are not being genuine.

5. **Assess their honesty:** Be cautious if you catch them in frequent lies or notice a lack of transparency. Dishonesty is a significant warning sign that someone may have ulterior motives.

6. **Evaluate their control tendencies:** Watch out for signs of controlling behavior, possessiveness, or attempts to isolate you from your loved ones. These can be indicators of an unhealthy and potentially manipulative relationship.

7. **Seek different perspectives:** Talk to friends and family about your new relationship. They may notice things you've missed or provide a more objective viewpoint.

8. **Take note of their response to boundaries:** Healthy relationships respect boundaries. If the person consistently disregards your boundaries or tries to push them, it could be a sign of manipulative behavior.

9. **Assess their empathy and compassion:** Observe their ability to empathize with others and show genuine concern. Lack of empathy or an excessive focus on themselves can be warning signs.

10. **Watch for love bombing:** Be cautious if the person showers you with excessive affection, compliments, and gifts early on in the relationship. Love bombing can be a tactic used to manipulate and gain control over someone.

Remember, these signs are not definitive proof of someone being a wolf in sheep's clothing, but they can serve as warning signs. Trust is earned over time, and it's essential to prioritize your emotional well-being and safety in any relationship.

Chapter 59

K arma, it's a bitch and I would never want to meet her.

In a relationship, you can hold a negative view of karma and express a desire not to encounter her. You see Karma is a concept rooted in various Eastern philosophies and religions, such as Hinduism and Buddhism. It suggests that our actions have consequences that can affect us in this life or future lives, depending on one's beliefs.

While the idea of karma is often associated with the notion of cause and effect, it's important to note that it is not a sentient being or force that actively seeks to punish or reward individuals. Karma is simply a system of understanding the moral and ethical implications of our actions.

If you feel that you have experienced negative consequences in your life and attribute them to karma, it may be helpful to examine your actions and behaviors to identify any patterns or areas for personal growth. Taking responsibility for your actions and making positive changes can contribute to a more fulfilling and harmonious life.

However, it's also important to recognize that life is complex, and not everything that happens can be neatly explained by the concept of karma. Many factors, including external circumstances and the actions of others, can influence our experiences.

If you're feeling overwhelmed by negativity or struggling with the consequences of your actions, it can be beneficial to seek support from friends, family, or professionals who can provide guidance and help you navigate through challenging times.

I lived that situation when I met karma and it's not a good feeling I believe it was my second marriage When I met her my second wife at the time didn't tell me I didn't notice that she was an alcoholic and I didn't know how to deal with it so that when I had an affair because all I wanted to do was to get away from that relationship in my mind after she broke her arm and her leg taking a shower I was afraid that I was going to get a phone call from the authorities that she was in a fatal accident he said the reason why was because she had five DWIs so with that said I wanted to add this chapter in my book. soon after my affair that's when I met karma and a bitch don't play real talk.

Chapter 60

Women beware of men that you bring into your home when you have children. When it comes to the safety and well-being of your children, it's important to exercise caution and make informed decisions. While it's not fair or accurate to generalize all men as potential threats, it's always a good idea to take certain precautions and be mindful of who you bring into your home.

Here are a few suggestions:

1. **Get to know the person:** Take the time to really get to know someone before inviting them into your home. Spend time together in public settings, engage in conversations, and observe their behavior and attitudes.

2. **Trust your instincts:** Trust your gut feelings when it comes to people. If something feels off or you have concerns about someone's character or intentions, it's important to take those feelings seriously.

3. **Background checks:** Consider conducting background checks, especially if you're considering a long-term commitment or introducing someone to your children. Background checks can provide information about someone's criminal history, helping you make a more informed decision.

4. **Talk to friends and family:** Seek input from trusted friends and family members who may have had interactions with the

person you're considering bringing into your home. They may offer valuable insights or share their own experiences.

5. **Open communication with your children:** Encourage open and honest communication with your children. Teach them about personal boundaries, what is appropriate behavior, and empower them to speak up if they ever feel uncomfortable or unsafe around anyone.

6. **Take things slow:** Rushing into a serious relationship or introducing someone to your children too quickly can increase the risks. Take your time to build trust and ensure the person is compatible with your family.

Remember, these suggestions are not foolproof, and there is no guaranteed way to eliminate all risks. However, by being vigilant, using common sense, and considering the safety of your children as a priority, you can minimize potential risks and create a safer environment for your family.

Chapter 61

Whatdo you do when you're in a relationship with a narcissistic person that wants to put tracking devices on your phone and cameras in your home.

If you suspect that you are in a relationship with a narcissistic person who wants to invade your privacy by putting tracking devices on your phone or installing cameras in your home, it's important to take steps to protect yourself and ensure your safety.

Here's what you can do:

1. **Assess the situation:** Carefully evaluate the signs and patterns of behavior that lead you to believe your partner is attempting to invade your privacy. Keep a record of any incidents or evidence that support your concerns.

2. **Reach out for support:** Talk to someone you trust, such as a close friend, family member, or counselor. Share your concerns and seek their advice and support. They can provide an objective perspective and help you navigate the situation.

3. **Set boundaries:** Clearly communicate your boundaries to your partner. Let them know that invading your privacy is not acceptable to you. Be assertive and firm, but also prioritize your safety. If you feel threatened or unsafe, it may be necessary to involve authorities or seek legal assistance.

4. **Secure your devices:** Take steps to secure your phone, computer, and other devices. Change your passwords frequently and make them strong with a combination of letters, numbers, and symbols. Enable two-factor authentication for your accounts, and consider using privacy settings to limit access to your personal information.

5. **Check for tracking devices:** If you suspect your partner has placed a tracking device on your phone or car, you can consult with a professional to conduct a thorough sweep of your belongings. They can help detect any hidden devices and remove them securely.

6. **Protect your home:** If you suspect your partner has installed cameras or surveillance equipment in your home without your consent, reach out to a professional to conduct a thorough inspection. They can help locate and remove any hidden devices.

7. **Seek professional help:** Consider consulting with a therapist or counselor who specializes in abusive relationships or narcissistic personality disorder. They can provide guidance, support, and strategies for dealing with the situation effectively.

8. **Develop an exit plan:** If you feel that your safety is at risk, it is essential to create a safety plan for leaving the relationship. This may involve reaching out to a domestic violence hotline or seeking assistance from local authorities. They can provide resources and guidance to help you leave safely.

Remember, it's important to prioritize your safety and well-being in such situations. If you feel threatened or in immediate danger, do not hesitate to contact emergency services in your area.

Chapter 62

I n some relationships one person once they're away and the other person wants their way how do you compromise.

Compromise is an important skill in any relationship, and it becomes especially important when one person is away and the other person wants their way.

Here are some steps you can take to find a compromise:

1. **Communication**: The first step is to openly communicate with each other about your desires, needs, and concerns. Make sure both parties have a chance to express their viewpoints without interruption.

2. **Active listening**: Practice active listening to understand each other's perspective. Try to put yourself in the other person's shoes and genuinely listen to their concerns and desires.

3. **Identify common ground**: Look for areas of agreement or common ground between both parties. This can serve as a starting point for finding a compromise.

4. **Brainstorm solutions**: Together, generate a list of potential solutions that could address both of your needs. Encourage creativity and open-mindedness during this process.

5. **Evaluate options**: Review the list of potential solutions and discuss the pros and cons of each option. Consider the feasibility, fairness, and practicality of each suggestion.

6. **Find a middle ground**: Seek a solution that incorporates elements from both parties' desires. Look for compromises that offer some degree of satisfaction to both individuals involved.

7. **Flexibility and generosity**: Be willing to be flexible and generous in your approach. Sometimes, it may require giving in a little more than you initially wanted to reach a compromise that satisfies both parties.

8. **Prioritize and negotiate**: If you still can't reach a compromise on every issue, prioritize the most crucial ones and be willing to negotiate on the less important ones. Find a balance that allows both individuals to feel heard and valued.

9. **Seek win-win outcomes**: Strive for win-win outcomes where both individuals feel that their needs are met and that the compromise is fair and reasonable.

10. **Revisit and adjust**: Revisit the compromise periodically to evaluate its effectiveness. If necessary, be open to adjusting and refining the compromise to better suit both individuals' evolving needs.

Remember, compromise requires a willingness to understand each other's perspectives, communicate effectively, and find solutions that satisfy both parties. It's a process that often requires patience, empathy, and a commitment to maintaining a healthy and balanced relationship.

Chapter 63

In relationships where the woman is carrying most of the weight and the man doesn't handle his part.

In relationships, it's important for both partners to contribute and share responsibilities in a fair and balanced manner. When one partner, regardless of gender, consistently carries most of the weight while the other fails to handle their part, it can lead to imbalances, resentment, and dissatisfaction.

If you find yourself in a situation where you feel that you are carrying most of the weight in the relationship, it's crucial to address the issue and communicate your concerns with your partner. Open and honest communication is key to resolving problems and finding solutions.

Here are some steps you can consider:

1. **Reflect on your needs and expectations**: Assess your own needs and expectations in the relationship. What specific areas or tasks are you hoping your partner will contribute to? Be clear about what you require for a healthy and balanced partnership.

2. **Communicate your feelings**: Choose an appropriate time and place to have a calm and honest conversation with your partner. Express your feelings and concerns in a non-accusatory manner. Use "I" statements to avoid sounding

confrontational. For example, say, "I feel overwhelmed with the household chores and would appreciate it if we could share the responsibilities more evenly."

3. **Be specific and provide examples**: Clearly articulate the areas where you feel your partner is not carrying their weight. Provide specific examples to illustrate your point. This can help your partner understand your perspective and the impact it has on you and the relationship.

4. **Listen to your partner**: Allow your partner to express their thoughts and feelings on the matter. They may have reasons or circumstances that explain their behavior. Encourage open dialogue and active listening to foster understanding and find common ground.

5. **Find solutions together**: Collaborate with your partner to find practical solutions. Brainstorm ways to divide tasks and responsibilities more equitably based on both of your strengths, interests, and schedules. This process should involve compromise and flexibility from both sides.

6. **Seek professional help if needed**: If the issue persists or becomes too difficult to resolve on your own, consider seeking the assistance of a relationship counselor or therapist. They can provide guidance and help facilitate effective communication and problem-solving.

Remember, relationships require ongoing effort and compromise from both partners. It's crucial to address imbalances and work together to create a mutually satisfying and supportive partnership.

Chapter 64

In relationships how to best communicate with each other without starting an argument.

Communication is key in any relationship, and it's important to approach it in a way that minimizes the chances of starting an argument.

Here are some tips on how to communicate effectively and avoid arguments:

1. **Choose the right time and place**: Find a calm and neutral environment where you both feel comfortable and can focus on the conversation without distractions. Avoid discussing important matters when either of you is stressed, tired, or in a rush.

2. **Use "I" statements**: Frame your thoughts and feelings using "I" statements rather than "you" statements. This approach helps avoid sounding accusatory or confrontational. For example, say "I feel upset when..." instead of "You always make me angry when..."

3. **Active listening**: Give your partner your undivided attention and actively listen to what they're saying without interrupting or planning your response in your head. Show empathy and understanding by paraphrasing or summarizing their points to ensure you've understood correctly.

4. **Stay calm and composed**: Keep your emotions in check during discussions. If you feel yourself becoming angry or frustrated, take a break and agree to resume the conversation later when you're both calmer. Remember, shouting or raising your voice rarely leads to productive communication.

5. **Focus on the issue, not the person**: Instead of attacking your partner's character or personality, focus on discussing the specific issue at hand. Address the behavior or situation that's causing concern rather than making personal attacks.

6. **Avoid blame and defensiveness**: Instead of assigning blame, approach the conversation with a problem-solving mindset. Be open to feedback and avoid becoming defensive. Remember, it's about finding a resolution together, not proving who's right or wrong.

7. **Use positive language**: Frame your concerns or requests in a positive and constructive manner. Instead of saying, "You never help with household chores," try saying, "I would appreciate it if we could share the responsibilities of household chores."

8. **Seek understanding**: Take the time to understand your partner's perspective, even if you disagree. Respect their opinions and try to find common ground or compromise. Remember, understanding doesn't necessarily mean agreement.

9. **Practice patience and empathy**: Recognize that you both have different backgrounds, experiences, and ways of thinking. Be patient with each other and try to see things from your

partner's point of view. Empathy can go a long way in defusing potential arguments.

10. **Take breaks if needed**: If the conversation becomes heated or you're unable to communicate effectively, it's okay to take a break and revisit the topic later. Sometimes, a little space and time can help both of you gain clarity and perspective.

Remember, effective communication takes practice and effort from both partners. By approaching discussions with respect, understanding, and a willingness to find common ground, you can foster healthier communication patterns and minimize the chances of starting an argument.

Chapter 65

W hen you're in a relationship and your narcissistic partner always says, 'What about me? If you loved me, you would understand me.

Dealing with a narcissistic partner can be challenging and emotionally draining. Narcissists often have an exaggerated sense of self-importance and can be highly demanding and self-centered in relationships. It's common for them to prioritize their own needs and expect their partners to constantly cater to them. Statements like "If you love me, you would understand me" are manipulative tactics commonly used by narcissists to guilt-trip their partners into complying with their desires.

However, it's important to remember that a healthy relationship should be based on mutual respect, understanding, and compromise. It's not healthy or fair for one person to consistently put their needs above their partner's and expect unconditional compliance.

Here are a few suggestions for dealing with a narcissistic partner:

1. **Establish boundaries:** Clearly communicate your needs and expectations in the relationship. Set boundaries that protect your well-being and ensure that your needs are also being met.

2. **Seek support:** Narcissistic relationships can be emotionally exhausting. Reach out to friends, family, or a therapist who can provide support, guidance, and a listening ear.

3. **Practice self-care:** Take care of your physical, emotional, and mental well-being. Engage in activities that bring you joy, reduce stress, and maintain your overall well-being.

4. **Develop a support network:** Surround yourself with supportive people who can offer you validation and understanding. Narcissistic partners often try to isolate their partners, so having a strong support network outside the relationship is crucial.

5. **Consider professional help:** If the relationship becomes toxic or emotionally abusive, it may be necessary to seek professional help or consider ending the relationship. A therapist can help you navigate the complexities of the relationship and provide guidance on the best course of action.

Remember, a healthy relationship should be based on mutual respect, reciprocity, and empathy. If you consistently feel unheard, devalued, or manipulated, it may be worth reevaluating the relationship and considering your own well-being.

Chapter 66

This is for women when in a relationship and sometimes you're tired from work you're stressed out and you partner wants to have sex but all you want to do is relax what you do.

In a situation where you're feeling tired, stressed, and simply want to relax, but your partner wants to have sex, it's important to communicate your needs and boundaries openly and honestly.

Here are a few suggestions on how to handle this situation:

1. **Communicate your feelings:** Express your current state of tiredness and stress to your partner. Let them know that you need some time to unwind and recharge. Honest communication is crucial for understanding each other's needs and finding a compromise.

2. **Offer alternative activities:** Suggest other ways of connecting and spending quality time together that don't involve sexual intimacy. For example, you can propose watching a movie together, taking a bath, or simply cuddling and talking. This allows you to relax while maintaining emotional closeness.

3. **Find a middle ground:** If you're open to some level of intimacy but not full sexual activity, communicate that to your partner. You can suggest engaging in activities like kissing, hugging, or giving each other massages that can help you feel connected without requiring a lot of energy.

4. **Prioritize self-care:** Explain to your partner the importance of self-care for your well-being. Emphasize that taking time to rest and destress will benefit both of you in the long run. Encourage them to support your need for relaxation and offer reassurance that you'll be more available for intimacy when you're in a better state of mind.

5. **Set boundaries:** It's essential to establish clear boundaries and respect each other's limits. Make sure your partner understands that your consent and comfort are important. If you're not in the mood for sexual activity, it's crucial that your partner respects your decision and doesn't pressure or guilt you into doing something you're not comfortable with.

Remember, open and respectful communication is key in any relationship. Both partners should strive to understand each other's needs, compromise, and find ways to support each other through different circumstances

Chapter 67

H ow can a woman and her children feel safe and secure in a toxic relationship.

Being in a toxic relationship can be a challenging and distressing situation, especially when there are children involved. It's important for a woman in such a situation to prioritize her safety and the safety of her children. Here are some steps that can help create a safer and more secure environment:

1. **Acknowledge the toxicity:** Recognize and accept that the relationship is toxic. Understand that it's not your fault and that you deserve better.

2. **Seek support:** Reach out to trusted friends, family members, or support groups who can provide emotional support and guidance. They can help you see things more clearly and offer practical advice.

3. **Develop a safety plan:** Create a safety plan that includes steps to protect yourself and your children. This may involve establishing a support network, identifying safe places to go in case of an emergency, and preparing essential documents and belongings to take with you if you need to leave quickly.

4. **Education and resources:** Educate yourself about domestic violence, its effects, and your rights. Research local resources

such as helplines, shelters, and counseling services that can offer support and guidance.

5. **Document incidents:** Keep a record of any abusive incidents, including dates, times, and descriptions of what occurred. This documentation can be valuable if legal action is needed in the future.

6. **Restraining order:** If you feel that you and your children are in immediate danger, consider seeking a restraining order. Consult with a lawyer or a domestic violence advocate to understand the legal process and your options.

7. **Financial independence:** If possible, work towards financial independence. This may involve finding employment, seeking educational opportunities, or exploring community resources that can help you become self-sufficient.

8. **Professional help:** Consult with a therapist or counselor who specializes in domestic violence. They can provide guidance, emotional support, and help you develop coping strategies.

9. **Safety at home:** Take steps to ensure the physical safety of your home. Install security measures such as locks, alarms, and surveillance cameras. Consider changing locks if you're concerned about your partner's access.

10. **Trust your instincts:** Trust your gut feelings. If you feel unsafe, take immediate steps to protect yourself and your children, even if it means leaving the relationship.

Remember, leaving a toxic relationship can be a complex and challenging process. It's crucial to have a support network and access to resources to help you navigate this difficult journey.

How to recover after a toxic relationship.

Recovering from a toxic relationship can be a challenging and emotional process, but it's important to prioritize your well-being and take steps to heal.

Here are some suggestions to help you recover:

1. **Acknowledge your emotions:** Recognize and accept your emotions. It's normal to feel a range of emotions such as sadness, anger, confusion, or even relief. Give yourself permission to experience these emotions without judgment.

2. **Cut off contact:** If possible, cut off contact with your toxic ex-partner. This may include blocking their phone number, unfollowing them on social media, and avoiding places where you're likely to run into them. Creating distance will allow you to focus on your healing without their presence or influence.

3. **Seek support:** Reach out to friends, family, or a support group who can provide a safe space for you to express your feelings and gain perspective. Consider talking to a therapist or counselor who specializes in relationship trauma. Professional guidance can help you navigate the healing process more effectively.

4. **Practice self-care:** Focus on self-care activities that promote physical, emotional, and mental well-being. Engage in activities that bring you joy, such as exercising, practicing mindfulness

or meditation, journaling, spending time in nature, or pursuing hobbies and interests. Taking care of yourself will help rebuild your self-esteem and confidence.

5. **Reflect and learn:** Take time to reflect on the toxic relationship and identify patterns or red flags that you may have missed. It's essential to learn from the experience to avoid repeating similar patterns in the future. This self-reflection can also help you regain a sense of control and personal growth.

6. **Set boundaries:** Establish clear boundaries to protect yourself from future toxic relationships. Learn to recognize and communicate your needs, and surround yourself with people who respect and support your boundaries.

7. **Give yourself time:** Healing takes time, so be patient with yourself. Avoid rushing into a new relationship as a way to distract yourself or fill the void. Focus on your personal growth and rebuilding your life independently before considering a new partnership.

8. **Cultivate self-love and self-compassion**: Remind yourself that you deserve love, respect, and happiness. Practice self-love and self-compassion by treating yourself with kindness, forgiveness, and understanding. Challenge negative thoughts and replace them with positive affirmations.

Remember, recovery is a personal journey, and everyone's healing process is unique. Be gentle with yourself, and if needed, don't hesitate to seek professional help to support you along the way.

This is what happens when a partner separates you from your family and friends in a toxic relationship I know this because my best friend got into a relationship with a guy and the first thing he wanted to do was separate her from me and her family she couldn't go anywhere she couldn't do anything and then he started telling her how to dress and how she could not be on Facebook or any other platforms or regards to friends and family that was a big red flag so with that said here's more ...When a partner separates you from your family and friends in a toxic relationship, it can have significant negative effects on your well-being and overall life.

Here are some of the potential consequences:

1. **Isolation:** By isolating you from your loved ones, the toxic partner gains control over your social support network. This isolation can make you feel lonely, trapped, and emotionally dependent on the toxic partner. It becomes harder for you to seek help or guidance from people who care about your well-being.

2. **Loss of perspective:** Being cut off from family and friends can make it difficult to maintain a balanced perspective on the relationship. Toxic partners often manipulate and gaslight their victims, distorting their perception of reality. Without the input of trusted friends and family, it may be harder for you to recognize the unhealthy dynamics of the relationship.

3. **Emotional abuse:** Isolation is a common tactic used by abusers to gain power and control over their victims. In a toxic relationship, emotional abuse is likely to occur. This can involve verbal insults, put-downs, constant criticism,

manipulation, and controlling behavior. Over time, this can lead to a loss of self-esteem, increased anxiety, and depression.

4. **Dependence:** When you are separated from your support system, your dependence on your toxic partner may increase. This dependence can make it harder for you to leave the relationship and can lead to a cycle of abuse where the toxic partner exerts even more control over you.

5. **Limited resources:** By cutting you off from family and friends, the toxic partner may also restrict your access to financial resources, transportation, and other practical forms of support. This can make it more challenging for you to leave the relationship or seek help when needed.

If you find yourself in a situation where your partner is separating you from your family and friends, it is essential to recognize the signs of a toxic relationship and take steps to protect yourself. Reach out to trusted friends, family, or professionals who can provide support and guidance. Consider seeking help from a therapist or contacting local organizations that specialize in domestic violence or relationship abuse. Remember, you are not alone, and there are resources available to help you navigate your situation and move toward a healthier, more fulfilling life.

Chapter 68

In my book I talk about love shouldn't hurt but it doesn't only pertain to the heterosexual community it also pertains to the **LGBT** community so this is a chapter on that.

In this chapter I will be talking about Love Shouldn't Hurt: Embracing Love in the **LGBT** Community

Love shouldn't hurt in any context, including within the transgender community. Love, respect, and acceptance are fundamental aspects of healthy relationships and should be present regardless of a person's gender identity.

Transgender individuals deserve to be loved and supported just like anyone else. They should be able to express themselves authentically and be accepted for who they are without experiencing emotional, physical, or psychological harm. It is important to recognize and challenge any discriminatory attitudes, biases, or prejudices that may exist, and create an environment where transgender individuals can thrive and experience love without fear or harm.

It is also crucial to address the unique challenges and experiences faced by transgender individuals, such as gender dysphoria, discrimination, and social stigma. By promoting understanding, education, and empathy, we can foster a society that values and respects transgender individuals, allowing them to build healthy and loving relationships that are free from harm and domestic violence.

Love Beyond Boundaries: Nurturing Healthy Relationships in the LGBT Community

In this chapter, we explore the universal principle that love should not cause pain or suffering, extending our discussion to the LGBT (Lesbian, Gay, Bisexual, and Transgender) community. Recognizing that love is a fundamental human experience, we delve into the unique challenges and triumphs faced by individuals within the LGBT community. By shedding light on relationship dynamics, acceptance, and self-love, we aim to promote a deeper understanding of the importance of nurturing healthy connections in all spheres of love.

Section 1: Understanding the Diversity of the LGBT Community

1.1 Exploring Sexual Orientation and Gender Identity: An Overview

1.2 Overcoming Stereotypes and Prejudices: Breaking Down Barriers

1.3 Intersectionality: Recognizing the Overlapping Identities

Section 2: Love and Relationships in the LGBT Community

2.1 Love Beyond Gender: Embracing Fluidity and Authenticity

2.2 Coming Out and Coming Together: The Journey of Self-Acceptance

2.3 Navigating Family and Society: Building Supportive Networks

2.4 Healthy Relationship Dynamics: Communication, Trust, and Boundaries

Section 3: Addressing Challenges and Promoting Well-being

3.1 Mental Health and Emotional Well-being: Addressing Stigma and Discrimination

3.2 Domestic Abuse and Intimate Partner Violence: Breaking the Silence

3.3 Advocacy and Legal Rights: The Fight for Equality

3.4 Celebrating Love and Resilience: Success Stories and Inspirational Figures

Conclusion

In closing, we emphasize the importance of recognizing that love has no boundaries, irrespective of sexual orientation or gender identity. By nurturing healthy relationships and promoting understanding, empathy, and acceptance, we can create a world where love is celebrated in all its forms. Through this chapter, we hope to inspire readers to embrace love as a transformative force that should never cause harm, fostering a society where love truly knows no bounds. ***Love Shouldn't Hurt***

Synopsis

"*Love Shouldn't Hurt*" is a powerful and thought-provoking book that explores the dark realities of abusive relationships while shedding light on the importance of healthy love and personal growth.

The story follows Alia, a young woman who finds herself trapped in a toxic relationship with her partner, James. As the narrative unfolds, readers witness the gradual deterioration of Alia's self-esteem, as well as the emotional, verbal, and physical abuse she endures. The book delves deep into the complexities of domestic violence, highlighting the manipulation, control, and fear that often accompany such relationships.

Amidst this harrowing journey, Alia discovers a glimmer of hope when she encounters a support group for survivors of domestic abuse. Through the guidance of empathetic individuals who have experienced similar hardships, she slowly begins to regain her strength and sense of self-worth. The book emphasizes the importance of support networks and resources available to those in abusive situations.

As Alia works to rebuild her life, the narrative explores the themes of healing, self-love, and personal transformation. It delves into the psychological aftermath of abuse, portraying the challenges and triumphs Alia faces as she relearns how to trust, love, and prioritize her own well-being.

"Love Shouldn't Hurt" is not only a gripping story of survival but also serves as a poignant reminder of the need for awareness and proactive measures against domestic violence. It aims to inspire readers to recognize the signs of abuse, offer support to survivors, and promote healthy relationships built on respect, kindness, and equality.

Through its compelling characters and raw emotions, this book encourages dialogue and reflection, fostering a greater understanding of the complexities surrounding abusive relationships. Ultimately, *"Love Shouldn't Hurt"* confronts the painful reality of domestic violence while advocating for a world where love is truly free from harm.

~~~ **End** ~~~

To my friend Alia,

we have stopped talking to each other on many occasions because I didn't like what you were going through in your toxic relationship Therefore I just wanted to send you this message so you can understand my feelings towards your relationship and our friendship.

Our best friendship over your toxic relationship and you chose your toxic relationship over our best friendship.

going through a difficult time in your friendship. It can be challenging when a friend prioritizes a romantic relationship over other relationships in their life. However, I understand you are in love.

It's important to remember that everyone has the right to make their own choices regarding their relationships. While it may be disappointing or hurtful that your friend has chosen to prioritize their romantic relationship over your friendship, it's crucial to respect their decision. Relationships can be complex, and there may be factors and dynamics at play that you're not fully aware of.

Instead of viewing it as an either-or situation, try to have an open and honest conversation with your friend. Share your feelings and concerns, expressing your desire to maintain a strong and supportive friendship. Make sure to listen to their perspective as well, as understanding their point of view can help you gain insight into their choices.

Ultimately, it's up to you to decide how to move forward. You may need to reevaluate your expectations and boundaries within the friendship. If you find that the toxicity of their romantic relationship is negatively impacting your well-being, it might be necessary to distance yourself for your emotional health.

Remember, friendships can evolve and change over time. It's natural for people to prioritize different aspects of their lives at different times. While it may be difficult, it's important to accept that your friend's choices are their own, and they may not align with what you hoped for in the friendship.

About the Author

Hello everyone, my name is Benjamin Holland, a.k.a. Dr. B.

C an you imagine a little black boy who was tortured by his mother? He and his sister... Can you imagine a little black boy who didn't know how to read or write because his family was moving all the time? Can you imagine a little black boy who learned how to read and write from billboards and street signs because he was always on the road? But he overcame all of those adversities to work at the Boeing company and retire as a team leader.

He remembers the times when he was in high-level meetings regarding what was going on in the 737 program. He used to look around the room sometimes and didn't see anyone who looked like him. He used to excuse himself a lot and go to the bathroom to cry, but then he had to pick himself back up and go back into these meetings because he was very good at what he did.

He graduated from Seattle Central Community College in 1978 after attending Olympic College and playing junior college football. He also played semi-pro football. But after that, he needed to get his life together, and that's when he joined Boeing.

He believes he was about 18 when he joined. He remembers after graduating from Seattle Central Community College with a welding degree, his first job was at Bethlehem Steel. He worked there for two weeks, and they had him sweeping and cleaning out pits. He went to the supervisor and said, "I'm a journeyman welder, not a sweeper." One day, he got to work, was called into the office, and they told him that he was let go. He's been asked, "Am I laid off? Am I fired? What does 'let go' mean?" They said, "We're just going to let you go." He was upset, but he didn't give up. At that moment, he went straight up the street to Boeing. At that time, at Boeing, you filled out a card, and then they would call you. But before he got out the door, a man came out and called his name, saying, "We want to make you an offer." Three hours later, he was hired. Know this: He is a journeyman welder. His white counterparts were grade eight, and he was a grade eight. They couldn't stand it. He had to prove himself. Time after time, he welded on the Minuteman missile, the MX missile, and several other secret projects.

He remembers one time he had to take a test because, at that time at Boeing, there were Air Force inspectors. There was a man called Danny Polly; his brother was a supervisor, and his other brothers were supervisors. He took the test alongside him, and he failed while he passed. He thought in his mind, "That was unfair." So, he talked to his supervisor, and he wanted to have all of the Air Force inspectors there. He wanted his supervisor to be there when they took the next test. During that next test, he hand-carried his results to the lab, and he passed with flying colors. Mr. Danny felt really bad. With that said, he fought every single day at Boeing. He had to endure racism; he was called "Nigga" so many times that he thought it was his name. But the worst part was when he worked in Auburn, Washington, at the Boeing clinic. When he went to the bathroom, there was a racial slur written all over the walls. He was afraid, but he was still young. That said, he overcame everything.

At one point, his supervisor came to him and told him that they had to downgrade him from a grade eight to a grade one. That bothers him because they were laying off all the welders since the Minuteman and the MX program were over. So, he took the grade one as a sweeper. But he told himself, "If I'm going to be a sweeper, I'm going to be the best sweeper they've ever seen." And that's what he did. Then, he moved up from that to a coordinator and a team leader.

With that said, he never gave up because they were trying to break him, just like his mother and his grandma tried to break him. But he never gave up...

That little black boy was me!

www.ingramcontent.com/pod-product-compliance
Lightning Source LLC
Chambersburg PA
CBHW021634120626
46545CB00002B/532